The Laughing Guide to Change

The Laughing Guide to Change

*Using Humor and Science to Master Your
Behaviors, Emotions, and Thoughts*

Ora Prilleltensky and
Isaac Prilleltensky

ROWMAN & LITTLEFIELD
Lanham • Boulder • New York • London

Published by Rowman & Littlefield
An imprint of The Rowman & Littlefield Publishing Group, Inc.
4501 Forbes Boulevard, Suite 200, Lanham, Maryland 20706
www.rowman.com

Unit A, Whitacre Mews, 26-34 Stannary Street, London SE11 4AB

British Library Cataloguing in Publication Information Available

Library of Congress Cataloging-in-Publication Data

Names: Prilleltensky, Ora, 1959- author. | Prilleltensky, Isaac, 1959- author.
Title: The laughing guide to change : using humor and science to master your behaviors, emotions, and thoughts / Ora Prilleltensky, Isaac Prilleltensky.
Description: Lanham, Maryland : Rowman & Littlefield, [2019] | Includes bibliographical references and index.
Identifiers: LCCN 2018032965 (print) | LCCN 2018035041 (ebook) | ISBN 9781475825787 (electronic) | ISBN 9781475825763 (cloth : alk. paper)
Subjects: LCSH: Change (Psychology) | Laughter.
Classification: LCC BF637.C4 (ebook) | LCC BF637.C4 P754 2019 (print) | DDC 158.1—dc23
LC record available at https://lccn.loc.gov/2018032965

∞™ The paper used in this publication meets the minimum requirements of American National Standard for Information Sciences Permanence of Paper for Printed Library Materials, ANSI/NISO Z39.48-1992.

Printed in the United States of America

To Beacon, our adorably misbehaved grand dog, who refuses to change

Beacon with Elizabeth, our daughter in law.

Contents

Preface

Do you experience stress? Are you interested in happiness and well-being? Are there things you want to change in your life? If you answered yes to any of these questions, you need to read this book. If you answered no to any of them, you're in denial, and don't even think of putting it down.

Most of us would like to change something about our lives. In fact, many of us have tried but given up in frustration. Change efforts usually fail because of four reasons: 1) lack of specific skills to engage in the change process, 2) strategies of change that don't appeal to people, 3) difficulty in persevering, and 4) lack of a meaningful goal. The key is to learn *specific skills* that *appeal to you* and can be *easily applied* to a *meaningful goal*.

There are multiple avenues to change, but not all of them will appeal to you; therefore, you have to find ways that are interesting, easy, and appealing. In this book we present a menu of options to engage in meaningful change. Specifically, we introduce three drivers of change: *behaviors*, *emotions*, and *thoughts*. Each driver of change contains two specific skills. We cover six skills aimed at helping you change. By giving you ample choices of where to get started, we're pretty confident that at least one of them will get you going. You start with one and then leverage other drivers and skills of change. This will result in synergy that will propel and sustain change.

In addition to *specific skills* that *appeal* to you, are *easy* to implement, and pertain to a *meaningful goal*, we believe change can be facilitated by humor and fun. There is no question that we take ourselves way too seriously. We submit that if we're willing to look at ourselves through a comic mirror, a lot of our defenses will come down, and change will be much easier. To lead by example, Isaac offers in this book multiple examples of self-deprecation, ranging from his girly voice to the size of his ears and his neurotic habits.

There is evidence that humor facilitates learning and psychological well-being.[1] In this book, we combine our love of humor with our love of well-being. We've been writing about well-being for the last twenty-five years. In the last few years, Isaac has also been writing about the funny side of life. His humor pieces have appeared in the *Miami Herald* and *Miami Today*, and most recently in his first humor book, *The Laughing Guide to Well-Being*.[2] The present book is part of a trilogy. *The Laughing Guide to Well-Being* combines humor with science to help you become happier and healthier. *The Laughing Guide to Change* uses humor and science to master your behaviors, emotions, and thoughts. Finally, *The Laughing Guide to a Better Life* is about improving yourself, your relationships, and your surroundings.

Each chapter of this book consists of two sections: the "Learning Side" and the "Laughing Side." In the former, we introduce specific skills that apply to a wide range of issues, for instance, relationships, work, stress, and physical and emotional well-being. In the latter, we reinforce the learning through humor.

There is research, which we take very seriously, that humor can reinforce the learning process. This is why we call our method *smarter through laughter*. At the beginning of each chapter you'll learn two specific skills associated with a driver of change. For example, in the first chapter, you'll learn how to set a goal and create a positive habit. These skills pertain to the first driver of change: behaviors. The first part of each chapter is based on scientific research. The second part is based on laughter.

The premise of *smarter through laughter* is that you learn better when you feel relaxed and happy. Positive moods and emotions open our mind to new ways of thinking. Humor generates happy moods, which in turn increase our psychological flexibility. Through satire we learn to poke fun at ourselves and entertain new possibilities we hadn't thought about before. Unfortunately, the potential of humor to help people change and improve their well-being has not been fully realized. We hope this book makes you laugh and helps you change. If you do one, we'd be ecstatic. If you do both, we'd be euphoric.

Finally, we'd like to say a few words about our coauthorship. We have been married for 35 years and have survived many adventures together, including three transoceanic moves; however, there is one thing we did that nearly killed us: writing a previous book on well-being. The fact that we also coauthored this book on well-being shows that a) we do not learn from experience, and b) we have way too much fun poking fun at one another.

Ora wrote most of the "Learning Side" of the book. She was also in charge of censoring some of Isaac's stories in the "Laughing Side." She did so primarily to make sure Isaac keeps his day job.

Acknowledgments

We gratefully acknowledge the work of our research team in building with us an intervention (www.funforwellness.com) based on the ideas reported in this book. We appreciate the contributions of Samantha Dietz, Adam McMahon, Nick Myers, and Carolyn Rubenstein. We also thank Patrizia Rizzo for help with the references and Yvette Carpintero for general support for Isaac as executive assistant extraordinaire. Michael Lewis of *Miami Today* graciously allowed Isaac to reproduce some humor columns previously published in his weekly newspaper. We also thank our editors at Rowman & Littlefield, Tom Koerner and Carlie Wall, for their support and guidance.

Chapter One

Drivers of Change

THE LEARNING SIDE

Changing Naturally

We all engage in feeling, thinking, and behaving. To change aspects of our life we do not like, we can work on our thoughts, emotions, or behaviors. We call them drivers of change. I can modify the environment to make it healthier. I can remove junk food from my house to eliminate temptations. I can increase my awareness about the health benefits of exercise. I can challenge negative perceptions about myself. Changes in any of the drivers can empower you to make improvements in areas of life that are important to you.

The advantage of using any of the drivers of change is that they occur naturally and don't require major life adjustments. The point is to experience success in one domain of life to increase your feeling of competency. Once you gain confidence it is easier to tackle other domains where the challenges are bigger. The key is to engage a driver of change that seems easy and appealing, and one you can use to advance a meaningful goal.

As you make your way through the book, you'll discover techniques that are easy to implement and follow. To facilitate learning and application, we break down each driver into two specific skills:

Behaviors

   Set a goal.
   Create positive habits.

Emotions

   Cultivate positive emotions.
   Manage negative emotions.

Thoughts

   Challenge negative assumptions.
   Write a new story.

Each chapter deals with a different driver of change and its corresponding skills. In this chapter, we provide an overview of the three drivers. Following the "Learning Side," we reinforce the lessons through the "Laughing Side."

People change in different ways. As a result, we must offer them more than one way to improve their well-being. Some begin the journey of change by rewarding themselves for small gains; others enter a new phase of their lives through careful thinking. Yet, others prefer to rearrange their environment to make it easy for them to achieve their goals.

The fact that different people resonate with different ways of changing encouraged us to integrate multiple methods. Some will start the process of personal growth through behavioral changes and others through cognitive means. The best we can offer people invested in personal growth is multiple points of entry.

Behaviors are the first driver of change. To *start*, *stop*, or *maintain* a behavior, we need to analyze its antecedents and consequences. Many people struggle with their weight. Eating is a behavior, so we can ask in what conditions or antecedents do I eat better or worse? What are the rewards that maintain my healthy or poor eating habits? Can I become a food detective and analyze in which situations I eat poorly and in which ones I eat healthy? What about exercising? To maintain a healthy weight we must eat well, but we must also engage in physical activity. In what conditions am I more likely to exercise? Is it when I'm by myself or with friends; in the morning or in the evening; indoor or outdoor? Can you build rewards that will encourage you to keep going? As we will see in the next chapter, the keys to behavioral change are to set realistic goals and to create positive habits. [1]

Emotions are the second driver of change. Many people overeat when they're feeling despondent. Negative emotions lead us to compensate through overeating. They also impact our thoughts and interactions with others. Managing negative emotions, as we'll see, is a valuable strategy for personal growth, but so is the cultivation of positive emotions. It is not enough to manage negative feelings; we also need to foster such positive emotional states as love, excitement, flow, and engagement. If we feel better, we're more likely to be better company and take initiative to go to the gym. We should not wait to have a major achievement in life to celebrate. Small deposits into our emotional bank account can bring many positive returns. [2]

The third powerful driver of change is thoughts. We talk to ourselves all the time. Some of us ruminate endlessly about our deficits, while others recall moments of happiness. Later in the book we review two essential strategies to leverage thoughts to our advantage: Challenge negative assumptions, and write a new story about ourselves. [3]

As you read the next chapters, think of which driver of change you can start using right away. Which one feels more natural to you? What about writing a new narrative or challenging negative assumptions about your life?

In the "Laughing Side" of each chapter, we review the drivers through humor. In general, you'll see that our problems derive from overdoing something, or not doing enough of it. Most neurotics like Isaac tend to worry too much, exercise too much, think about what they eat too much, work too much, plan too much, and overall obsess too much. On the other hand, some folks don't think enough about what they eat and don't pay enough attention to work, and overall they are clueless about their health and wellness. See if you find yourself, or anyone you know, in any of the stories. The motto of this book is *smarter through laughter*. If you can laugh about it, you can probably start changing it.

THE LAUGHING SIDE

Neurotic Life

Behavior is the first driver of change, and setting a goal is the first skill we should master. Controlling my neurosis (Isaac's) was never an explicit goal of mine, but it is about time.

When I was finishing my Ph.D. in psychology, I was also working a full-time job, raising a baby, and writing a dissertation on a tight schedule. Ora and I would not get much sleep because Matan, our son, would want to play in the middle of the night, and we had no idea how to say no, which, after 30 years, we still don't. This was in Winnipeg, the capital of Manitoba in Canada. In winter, the temperature was –40, and in summer there were 108 mosquitoes per square foot.

To make sure I completed my dissertation on time, I followed compulsively a tight schedule. I used to get up at 5 a.m., go down to the basement, and start typing. I wrote nonstop until 7 a.m. to make sure I achieved my word goal for the day. My obsessive–compulsive tendencies were only in embryonic form then. Throughout the years, I went on to obsess about not only writing, but also eating, exercising, going to the bathroom, taking out life insurance, and buying brown clothes, watches, shoes, and bags.

If having a goal is good for well-being, I figured having multiple goals would be even better. So, I outlined a life plan with multiple goals. First, stay out of jail. Second, avoid frost bites. Third, avoid mosquitoes. Fourth, avoid constipation. Fifth, get the heck out of Winnipeg.

To achieve my fifth goal, I tried to get an academic position, which I heard was good for types like me. But to get a job interview I needed to publish some academic papers. I focused so intently on publishing that one of my friends said I suffered from attention surplus disorder. I got an academic position, and off we went to Waterloo, Ontario, which, compared to Winnipeg, felt like the tropics. It took us eight years to realize we were still living in Canada and we were still freezing our butts off, so we moved as far away from Canada as possible.

We landed in Melbourne, Australia, just in time to welcome the new millennium. I went from a task-oriented culture to one where everyone was on long service leave longer than they were at their desks. What a concept! In Canada, I worked with very productive colleagues who only reinforced high work ethic. In Australia, I worked with wonderful colleagues who only reinforced the realization that I was an idiot for working so hard.

After three years in Australia trying to control my neurotic tendencies, I relented to my pathologies and moved back to North America, where I could wallow in self-pity for working so hard. We not only came back to a workaholic culture, but to Nashville no less, where other than country music, all there is to do is work. We went from a food mecca to a food desert. The nearest vegetarian restaurant in Nashville was in Asheville. We tried socializing, but that didn't work out so well. As a friend told me, "Nashville is a place that makes you feel more welcome than you really are."

After three years in Nashville, we were so desperate we were thinking of going back to Winnipeg. If that failed we could always move to Moldova and reclaim the land the Cossacks stole from my family during the Kishinev pogrom. After debating between Manitoba and Moldova, we moved to Miami.

Controlling your behavior in Miami is a matter of life and death. If you want to stay alive in Miami, you have to master your driving behavior. First, you have to control the automatic desire to move ahead when traffic lights turn green. Second, you have to count four cars that will cross in red in front of you. Third, if you don't want to be rear-ended, you have to accelerate when the light turns yellow. Finally, you have to learn a few choice words in Spanish to communicate with the drivers blocking intersections.

Miami is indeed a wonderful place to learn how to control your behavior. You have to unlearn everything you know about driving—unless, of course, you come from Latin America. I was born in Argentina and lived there for the first 16 years of my life, enough to mentor Messi, Maradona, and Pope Francis (Evita died before I was born). Given my Hispanic background you would have thought I'd know how to drive in Miami, but all I remember are some choice words I use in intersections.

But Miami is nothing if not entertaining. If you want to laugh with a purpose, Miami is an ideal setting, so much so that I decided to use some of my experiences to inform the *smarter through laughter* approach. Without humor, you can become depressed really quickly. In Miami, when it's not the drivers, it's rising sea levels. When it's not government corruption, it's Medicare fraud.

To survive in Miami, I started writing humor. Unexpectedly, in 2015 one of my pieces received Second Best Humorous Column by the National Newspaper Association (NNA), which encouraged me to use humor in this book. If you don't like the result, you can blame the NNA.

Male Emotional Brain Found in Garage

Managing your emotions is an essential part of improving your life. Unfortunately, most males have a hard time with it.

I, Isaac, envy my wife. When we go for walks with other couples she usually goes next to the woman, and I usually get stuck with the man. While the women get to talk about how they're feeling and how life is going, I get to hear exhilarating updates about garage renovations. From garage talk they move to the latest Harley-Davidson model, followed by an analysis of why the Marlins are still an awful team. If I get a lucky break my male companion will ask me how I'm doing, but I quickly learned that they have no interest whatsoever in the answer.

Male Friend: How are you doing?

Isaac: Well, as of late . . .

Male Friend (interrupting me): Great! Have you been to Home Depot lately? Weed and Feed is on sale.

This recurring and traumatic experience has led me to ponder the emotional development of the male species. If most males have the emotional brain of a pea and all they can talk about is completely devoid of depth, feelings, meaning, nuance, and commitment, where does that leave me?

I have an adorable and wonderful friend who can talk about nothing other than the state of his roof and the brake pads on his car. We used to go for walks together and he'd pick up old newspapers from the floor in case there were coupons for Home Depot.

The one emotion men do know how to express is anger. They're so detached from their feelings that, when something doesn't go their way, frustration quickly turns into aggression. Their inability to process the mildest threat leads to a complete meltdown. I know a specimen, other than Donald Trump, who when the world doesn't behave according to his whim, he goes into a predictable pattern: a) regression to prenatal stage, b) nonsensical verbiage, c) self-pity,

d) pouting, e) abusive language, f) threat of retaliation, and g) rant about lack of justice in the world.

In addition to anger, expressions of control, domination, and supremacy are pretty common among males. These might have been useful in the African Savanna, but someone forgot to mention that most of us are no longer running away from Tyrannosaurs. But even for those of us who did get the news, we still worry about a lot of stuff. In my dreams, I have some recurring fears:

1. I am late for my flight.
2. I find myself naked in a busy intersection.
3. I am not prepared to teach my class. (This one comes in several varieties: Someone assigned me to teach nuclear physics, Chinese, or organic chemistry.)
4. I lost my wallet.
5. I lost my bag.
6. I ate meat.
7. I am late paying my life insurance.

To cope with my fears, I obsessively plan. My life insurance policies are on automatic debit. It usually works, but I still have some primal fears of public shame, as in numbers 2 and 3. I thought of getting degrees in nuclear physics, Chinese, and organic chemistry, but my wife threatened to divorce me. To prevent the humiliation of number 2, I always leave home with my clothes on. Not only that, but I take a change of clothes as well.

Number 7 presents a unique challenge. I worry a lot about my family. This one is not hard to decipher. I lost my parents when I was eight years old. Both died in a car accident. It doesn't take a psychoanalyst to figure out I worry about death—my own and others'. Ora, my wife, uses a wheelchair, and she has a hard time getting up from bed, which is where I come in. The other night I woke up in a sweat thinking that if I die in the middle of the night of a heart attack she might not be able to get up the next day and would die from starvation; our son would become an orphan, and it is all *my fault*, and I'm not even alive to feel guilty— which is why I have never seen a life insurance policy I didn't like.

Existential Worries

If you're like most people, you probably spend quite a bit of time pondering the meaning of life. Does my existence matter? Why should I change? Most Americans are really concerned about these philosophical issues. In fact, the latest research shows that the average American spends increasingly more time each year asking existential questions. The time devoted to these concerns has gone up every year since 1649. Compared to that year, in 2017 the average American spent 3,278% more time thinking about the meaning of life.

We're now at an all-time high for pondering existential matters: Twenty-eight seconds per year. Research also shows these precious seconds are spent mostly by football fans after their teams lose. This is the time it takes them to get drunk.

In sharp contrast to the *average* person, the *neurotic* American spends 25 hours a day fretting and engaging in all kinds of cognitive errors. Neurotics like me worry about different things throughout the lifespan. For example, there are a number of serious prenatal concerns that neurotic babies experience in the womb, for example, lack of Wi-Fi spots. Their mothers are desperate to send ultrasound pictures to their parents, workmates, and Facebook friends. The neurotic unborn worries about that, increasing the chances of PTSMD (preterm social-media disorder). In addition, the unborn need access to e-mail. They need to know whether they got accepted into the most exclusive and ridiculously expensive college prep nursery. E-mail access for the unborn is a real priority in this country.

As an unborn, my primary concern was to beat 300 million sperm in the quest to fertilize an egg. Without a doubt, this is the most existential period of time for any sperm. Unless you reach your destination, you vanish into the black hole of fallopian tube history. Sperms can use intrauterine GPS technology to avoid traffic jams.

Once they come into the world, neurotic newborns have a lot to worry about. By the time they go to college, the SAT will have a music appreciation component, so they better master Mozart from a young age. In addition, newborns have to burp. At the end of the day, burping is the main reason for a baby's existence. Parents, grandparents, aunts, and uncles want baby to burp. If you want to win an election in this country, you better come up with a fast-acting burping formula. Neurotic parents will love you.

When I was a newborn, I had two main concerns: circumcision and feeling guilty for crying during the procedure.

By the time they reach infancy, neurotic kids need help with college applications. Now, to be sure, neurotics come in different forms. When I was an infant, instead of thinking about college I worried about the size of my ears. It was at that time that I started planning my move to Miami—plastic surgery capital of the world.

While the average toddler today is obsessed with Super Smash Bros. and Mario Kart 8, I was obsessed with Fascism, Anti-Semitism, and diverticulitis. Call me paranoid, but you didn't grow up in Argentina, surrounded by dictators, Nazis, and red meat.

Since all adolescents are neurotic, it's easy to understand them. They're totally obsessed with the elimination of two things: zits and embarrassing erections.

Now, the largest portion of the population is obviously adults. They're all neurotic and addicted to Apple products like iPhones, iPads, Apple Watches, and, the latest, i-enemas. When they're not obsessing about Apple products and standing in line to buy the latest gadget, they're having sex, texting while driving, watching football, or drinking beer.

The final neurotic group is senior citizens, who worry about two existential threats: erections and memory. Male senior citizens are desperately trying to get an erection with large quantities of Viagra, while their female partners are desperately trying to remember what an erection looks like.

If you want to improve your life, you're going to have to change some thinking patterns and get a hold of these anxieties. Stick around for the rest of the book.

Chapter Two

Behaviors

THE LEARNING SIDE

If you want to improve your well-being you have to start by examining your behavior. Do the things you do contribute to your well-being? Do some of your habits and behaviors interfere with how you want to lead your life?

When you think about it, it seems puzzling that anyone would act against his or her best interests; however, some people sabotage their long-term health and happiness. It seems counterintuitive that people would do things like eating junk food or drinking too much, even though they know that it is bad for them. Some of us don't exercise or pay our bills on time, even though doing so is clearly the better choice.

Clearly, many of our behaviors are inconsistent with our long-term goals and ultimate health and happiness. This is because it is often more rewarding to indulge our sweet tooth, get up later than we should, or watch TV instead of paying bills. We often do what is easy and pleasurable in the short term even though we know that we will pay a price for it later. [1]

Luckily, people can take active steps to change their behavior. Many positive health behaviors are within your control. These behaviors have a huge influence on your health and wellness. Research on self-control has taught us that regulating our behavior is a learned skill that improves with practice.

Training ourselves to do more of what we want and less of what we don't want can also help us feel happier. In fact, changing what you do is a better path to happiness than trying to change how you feel. [2] In this chapter, we focus on two behavioral skills that can help you in your personal growth: set a goal and create positive habits.

Set a Goal

A goal is something you aspire to, a desired state of affairs in your future; however, not all goals are created equal, and people often choose goals that are not necessarily right for them. [3] The following exercise will help you see the difference between goals that are a good fit versus those that are not.

Bring to mind a goal you consider important and are trying to accomplish. What is your motivation for accomplishing this goal? Why are you doing it? Place a checkmark next to each sentence that applies to you.

7

My goal:

_____

I work on this goal because:

1. I enjoy the challenge.
2. It is important for my health and well-being.
3. I find it interesting.
4. Others want me to do it.
5. It's fun to do.
6. It is meaningful to me.
7. I feel guilty if I don't do it.
8. I believe it is truly important to me.
9. I think this is what successful people do.
10. It'll make me rich one day, even though I hate doing it now.
11. Everyone in my family accomplishes this.
12. I will feel like a loser if I don't do it.
13. It's related to something I really value and desire.

Can you see which statements belong together? Can you put them in two different categories? What would you call category A? What would you call category B?

_____

As I work on this goal . . .

1. I'm totally absorbed and barely notice the passage of time.
2. I clearly see its connection to other things I value.
3. I never want to get started.
4. I feel totally engaged.
5. I have a sense of meaning and accomplishment.
6. I feel really good about doing it, even if it's not fun.
7. I keep dragging my feet.
8. I am motivated to stick with it even when the going is tough.
9. I feel a sense of pressure.
10. I think about how I would rather do something else.
11. I think it's not me.

Can you put these sentences in two different categories? What did you learn from this exercise about your own goals?

You are more likely to accomplish a goal when you find it *meaningful* or *enjoy working toward it*. Conversely, goals that are not personally significant are less likely to be accomplished.[4] You need to work on a goal that is self-concordant, not a goal that is imposed on you by pressure or social convention.[5] In other words, you need to work on a goal you consider important and you enjoy working toward. If you are still unsure if the goal you are trying to pursue is a self-concordant one, ask yourself the following questions:

1. Do I enjoy the process of working toward this goal? Do I find it interesting and engaging?
2. If it is not particularly enjoyable or interesting, is it related to something I truly value and is important to me?
3. Will accomplishing this goal lead to greater health and happiness even if the process is difficult?
4. Is it related to who I truly am and what I really want in life?

It is important to keep in mind that the path to a personally significant future is not always intrinsically rewarding. Reaching a desired state of affairs may require you to cut down on desserts, study even if you don't feel like it, or curb your spending to save for the future. You want the ultimate outcome of better health, a valued degree, or future financial security, but you need to overcome the desire for immediate gratification. You need to manage your behavior so that it serves rather than hinders your long-term goal.[6]

You also need to ensure that what you are striving for is realistic, achievable, and within your control. If you are a student and you want to earn an A in calculus, this is not fully within your control. Nonetheless, your goal of improving your grade entails a series of steps that you do have control over. For example, you can increase the time you study calculus, go for extra help if you need it, or review your notes on a daily basis. These behaviors are realistic, within your control, and consistent with the goal of a higher grade.

Self-change is a fascinating field of study with highly practical applications. There is a lot of evidence-based information on a) how to choose goals that are right for you, b) how to increase your chance of achieving them, and c) how to strengthen your resolve in the face of temptations. Hiccups and setbacks are bound to occur, so planning for them should be part of your roadmap. When it comes to setting goals, consider the following rules of thumb.

Remind Yourself Why This Is Important to You

Establish a clear connection between your ultimate long-term, self-concordant goal and what you need to do to advance it. Reminding yourself why you want to be healthy—for yourself, your spouse, or your kids—can help you as you struggle with temptations. Reminding yourself of a personally meaningful future state can also help you struggle through a difficult course you don't enjoy. This can also curtail frivolous spending and avoid family conflict.

Frame Your Goal in the Positive

For many people, reaching a desired state of affairs entails reducing or eliminating a certain behavior, for instance, eating junk food or spending too much time on Facebook. Even if your goal is to eliminate a bad habit or reduce a certain behavior, your ultimate long-term goal should be stated in the positive. What will your life be like when you eliminate this problem behavior? What will you be thinking, feeling, and doing? Thinking about the healthy opposite of your problem behavior[7] can inspire you a lot more than simply thinking about its absence.

Deal with ambivalence

We are often ambivalent about making a change in our life. We want to accomplish a certain goal but may be reluctant to do what is needed to accomplish it. Many problem behaviors are very rewarding in the short term. You want to improve your diet but loath giving up your favorite comfort food. You want to save money for graduate school but enjoy spending your disposable income on clothes and dinners out.

Behavior change experts[8] suggest a systematic approach to tackling ambivalence by evaluating the costs and benefits of behavior change. This requires considering the pros and cons of making the change, both in the short term and in the long term. If you conclude that the benefits of changing are greater than the costs, you've already made some progress. You have increased your commitment to following through with your plan and overcoming potential barriers. Do the following exercise:

My goal is:

_____

What are the short-term advantages of making this change?

_____

_____

_____

What are the short-term disadvantages?

_____

_____

_____

What are the long-term advantages of making this change?

_____

_____

_____

What are the long-term disadvantages?

_____

_____

_____

Focus on the Process of Change Rather Than the Outcome

This may seem counterintuitive. Shouldn't you have a specific outcome in mind, a benchmark that will be an indication of whether you have met your goal? Consider the student striving for an A in calculus. The end result is not fully within their control, just as achieving a promotion or saving a marriage is not fully and exclusively within one's control.

By focusing on the process rather than on the outcome, you can take steps that are fully within your control, provided they are framed the right way. What is one step you can take that will bring you closer to your desired goal? This one step can be your first subgoal.

Make Your Step or Subgoal SMART

Whether your goal is to improve your health, your relationships, or your finances, or to become more productive, more sociable, or more involved in the community, you need to begin by identifying one specific step you can take toward your goal. In the absence of specific, actionable steps, your plan for self-improvement will remain vague and unfulfilled. The SMART acronym, popular in the business word, stands for Specific, Measurable, Attainable, Relevant, and Time-Bound.[9]

For example, Ora's wellness goal of daily meditation can be framed in the following way: "Meditate a minimum of fifteen minutes at least four times a week for the next three weeks." This is a SMART goal: Specific, Measurable, Attainable, Relevant, and Time-Bound. The goal is specific—it clearly spells out what needs to be done. It is measurable because I (Ora) can easily keep track of the number of times I meditate each week and for how long.

The goal is attainable; not only is it within my control, but also I purposefully made it easy by starting with fifteen minutes four times a week. I preferred to experience success and then build on it rather than setting a more ambitious goal and feeling down if I fail to achieve it. The goal is highly relevant to my well-being.

As someone whose mobility and range of movement is severely restricted due to muscular dystrophy, I particularly appreciate the opportunity to improve well-being through mindful meditation. Finally, the goal is time-bound, as I set it for a period of three weeks. I decided that is enough time to see if it's something I want to continue and if I want to increase its frequency and duration.

What about you?

My long-term goal is:

_____

_____

My first SMART subgoal is:

_____

_____

Make a Plan for Implementing Your Goal

Whereas you are less likely to achieve a goal that was not a good fit in the first place, adopting a self-concordant goal is no guarantee for success.[10] When your goal involves something you love to do, simply making the decision might be enough for you to act on it.

But what if you want to write a book but rarely find the time to write even though you enjoy it? Many of us face competing demands on our time and may give up on activities that are not absolutely necessary, despite the meaning or pleasure we derive from them.[11] An even greater challenge is when our long-term goal requires us to do things we find difficult or don't really feel like doing.

There is considerable evidence that forming a specific plan for implementing your goal can increase your chance of achieving it.[12] An implementation plan will specify exactly where, when, and how you will engage in goal-directed behavior. It will include what you will do, where you will do it, and when you will do it. Implementation plans are particularly important for behaviors you find difficult to initiate due to either external (i.e., competing time demands) or internal (i.e., it's not fun to do) constraints.

Implementation intentions work by making the behavior you need to engage in more automatic and, thus, more likely to occur. By articulating the specific context in which to engage in this behavior, this context is your cue that your goal-directed behavior is now called for.[13]

For example, I find it easier and more productive to meditate first thing in the morning. I found that if I don't do it early in the morning, I am a lot less likely to do it at all. My goal of meditating for fifteen minutes a day can be stated as such: "I will meditate in my study right after I drink my morning cup of hot water and lemon."

We get up early, and as soon as I'm showered and dressed I crave my hot water and lemon. This is how I start the day. By tying my meditation routine to this ingrained and enjoyable habit, I am maximizing the likelihood that I will do it. Meditation comes after water and lemon but before coffee and fruit.

In multiple studies, and across various domains, implementation plans have facilitated engagement in goal-directed behavior.[14] For instance, students instructed to write a plan specifying when, where, and how they would work on a report were more likely to complete it than those who did not write such a plan.[15] Similarly, individuals who intended to exercise and made a specific plan of where, when, and how they will do so had superior results to a comparable group of nonplanners.

Implementation intentions are even associated with a higher likelihood of finally going for a colonoscopy[16] or recycling.[17] Implementation plans can run on automatic pilot due to their "if then" component.[18] If X happens, it is time to do Y. If my roommate is out for the evening, I'll immediately open my books and review for class. If I finish my work, I'll clear my desk before leaving the office. If I finish my hot water and lemon, I will meditate.

Anticipate Barriers and Make a Plan to Overcome Them

Given a choice, would you rather:

1. Fantasize about a rosy future when your valued goals are accomplished?
2. Envision what stands in the way of accomplishing a valued goal?

The answer to this question surely seems like a no-brainer. Who wouldn't prefer the rosy future fantasy? As it turns out, the answer to this question depends on what you're trying to achieve. If you are procrastinating on a project or struggling to stick to an exercise routine, it's certainly more fun to fantasize that tomorrow, next week, or next month, you will have the willpower to accomplish your goal. This can certainly make you feel good—almost as if you've already accomplished your goal. Nonetheless, it will do little for your goal and deflate you in the long run.[19]

Many a motivational speaker has pumped up his audience with positive thinking messages: "Thinking negatively will only bring you down. Thinking positively will make your dream a reality. Don't think of barriers; just tell yourself that you can do it!" This may be a good message if you are the speaker charging big bucks for your talk. But if you are the sucker parting with your hard-earned money to lap up this happy-inducing message, you should think again.

In fact, you are much better off adding a healthy dose of realism, along with a sprinkling of pessimism. Thinking about what stands in the way of your goal may not fix your mood, but it can fix your plan. [20] Provided your goal is realistic to begin with, envisioning a barrier can help you plan for ways to overcome it. In study after study and across multiple domains, envisioning a barrier, followed by a plan for addressing it, has facilitated goal accomplishment.

Complete the following exercise:

What is your long-term goal?

_____

_____

_____

What is one step you can take toward your goal?

_____

_____

_____

What is your implementation plan?

_____

_____

_____

What will you do and how will you do it?

_____

_____

_____

Where and when will you do it?

_____

_____

Make an if-then plan (e.g., "If I feel like a snack, I will eat an apple," or "If it's 4 pm, I will go to the library to study for an hour").

_____

_____

What obstacle might get in the way of acting on your goal (e.g., "I don't have apples at home," or "My boyfriend will want to hang out with me when I'm about to go to the library and I won't want to say no")?

_____

_____

What can you do to address this obstacle? What plan can you put in place (e.g., "I will add apples to my shopping list and if I still run out, I'll eat a banana or orange instead," or "I'll tell my boyfriend ahead of time that I can't hang out between 4 and 6 p.m. because I have to go to the library to study")?

_____

_____

_____

Create Positive Habits

A four-year-old boy is seated at a table. He is presented with a plate containing a single marshmallow and offered the following choice: Eat the fluffy, fragrant marshmallow now or wait fifteen minutes until the experimenter returns with another one. If the treat is left uneaten by the time the experimenter comes back, the little boy will be rewarded with another marshmallow. The experimenter exits the room, leaving the child in front of the marshmallow. Can he do it? Will he gobble it up now or double his prize by waiting fifteen minutes? Will he manage to exert enough self-control and hold out for the larger reward?

This classical experiment has been repeated time and time again since it was initially conducted more than fifty years ago.[21] In fact, googling "marshmallow test" or "marshmallow study" will send you to multiple clips and descriptions of this experiment. A friend of ours, a retired teacher, recently wondered if her three-year-old granddaughter is old enough to be presented with a similar dilemma.

The fascination with this simple experiment is due to its ability to predict future behaviors that have nothing to do with marshmallows but much to do with future health, educational attainment, and earning potential. It turns out that the ability to delay gratification and exert self-control as a four-year-old is a stable characteristic that serves you well in the future. We are often our own worst enemies, as the saying goes, due to poor impulse control and difficulty managing our own behavior. Hence, an abundance of self-control and perseverance is associated with multiple positive outcomes in various domains of life.[22]

However, there is good news, even for those of us who would've surely gobbled up the marshmallow. You may be highly disciplined in one domain but struggle with self-control in a different domain. For example, getting yourself to study more may be relatively easy, while getting yourself to eat better may be more difficult.

More importantly, there is much we can do to help ourselves act in ways that can advance our long-term goals and future health and happiness. This is because self-control is a skill that can be learned and cultivated.[23] The more we practice it, the better we get at it. The more informed we are about the obstacles that get in its way, the more we can do to address them.

Know Your Habits

We often do things automatically, without being fully aware of our actions. When a habit is established, enacting it becomes rather automatic and outside of our awareness. This is true for healthy, as well as unhealthy, habits. If you have established a habit of going to the gym first thing in the morning, you probably put your gym clothes on as soon as you get out of bed. You go to the bathroom, brush your teeth, and leave for the gym. If you follow the same routine every day it runs on automatic pilot. You don't have to think and plan to carry it out. In fact, you can go through your morning routine of getting ready for, and even driving to, the gym while planning for an important meeting you will have later that day. The automaticity of your morning routine enables you to do it so effortlessly and seamlessly that your mind is freed up to do something else.

The problem is that such unhealthy habits as snacking on potato chips as soon as you come home also become automatic and outside of your awareness. Consider the case of Florence, a middle-aged preschool teacher. Florence has had an issue with weight her entire life. Diabetes runs in her family and she grew up on meat and potatoes—a common staple of the standard American diet, rightfully referred to by its acronym, "SAD." Florence is tired and hungry by the time she comes home from work. All she wants to do is satisfy her hunger and relax quietly in front of the TV.

In fact, Florence follows the same routine every day after work. As soon as she gets home she turns on the TV, grabs a bag of chips from the cupboard, and sits down to watch her favorite prerecorded program. This well-established habit is now out of her awareness; she does it automatically without paying attention to what she is doing.

Since many of our behaviors run on automatic pilot and out of our awareness, we need to adopt a scientific approach and gather data about the behavior we want to change. If you have a decent salary but are always short on cash toward the end of the month, you need to keep track of your spending. If you want to improve your diet but keep eating junk food, you need to keep a food journal and record everything you put in your mouth. What you find may surprise you and even make you uncomfortable. *Am I really spending all that money on ice coffee and makeup? Did all this food really pass my lips? Have I only studied for forty-five minutes the entire evening?*

At times, simply recording your behavior can help you change it, as it draws your attention to what you are actually doing. This awareness is an important first step in taking charge of your own behavior. If your actual behavior does not match your expectations of yourself, this may be an intervention in and of itself.

Behavior change experts suggest keeping track for about a week to get an accurate picture of your target behavior.[24] This is no easy feat, as there are bound to be times when it will be inconvenient to do so, or you will forget or simply won't feel like it. Make your recording as easy as possible and tell yourself to keep at it. Awareness is your friend, and good friends tell the truth even when it is not pretty.

Detect Your Triggers and Rewards

Whether we notice it or not, every behavior takes place within a certain context.[25] The behavior is triggered by something: a place we are at; a certain time of the day; the presence of another person; or even our own thoughts, feelings, and sensations. These triggers act as cues that a certain behavior should follow even if we are unaware of it.

Isaac and I stick to a healthy, predominantly vegan diet and have been doing so for many years. Last week we had a meeting at our house. Among other refreshments, we served rugalach, a type of cookie I find particularly irresistible. The day after the meeting I was hungry for a midmorning snack and checked out the fridge. In addition to freshly cut veggies and assorted nuts, there was a plate of leftover rugalach. Without giving it much thought I reached for one and down it went. The cue was there, and the behavior followed.

An e-mail advertising a clearance sale at your favorite clothing store will probably be followed by clicking and spending. A Facebook message that a close friend updated his status may distract you from your work. In addition to cues in our environment, we respond to internal cues. Many people indulge in comfort food when they feel sad, lonely, or bored. Our thoughts also cue us to behave in certain ways, for instance, the student who doesn't raise her hand in class because she thinks her answer may be wrong and being wrong is unacceptable.

If your goal is to change a certain behavior, it is helpful to keep track of what comes immediately before that cues you to behave in a certain way. This will give you important information about triggers you can either remove (give those leftover cookies away), add (a water bottle on your desk), or change (unsubscribe from websites) to make it easier for you to act according to your plan.

What comes before the behavior serves as a trigger, whereas what comes immediately after it serves as reinforcer. When something you do is followed by something you like, you will do it again and again. This is a simple behavioral principle that you surely already know. Nonetheless, we often fail to consider how we inadvertently reward ourselves for the very behavior we want to change. The yummy-looking free sample in the supermarket, the blinking sale sign, and the Facebook message signal the prospect of a reward. Our brain responds to such signals with a huge release of dopamine, a neurotransmitter that turns us into reward-seeking machines.[26]

The reward of the yummy food, new dress, or entertaining Facebook post serves as immediate reinforcement for our indulgent behavior, even though it clearly does not serve us in the long run. Later, the hot thought of "I gotta have it and I gotta have it now" will be replaced with the rational cold thought that this behavior is an obstacle to your long-term goal. It will bring to mind the cholesterol clogging your arteries, the dress clogging your closet, and the time wasted on Facebook.

A healthy dose of self-critique may lead you to consider how you can reward yourself for behaviors that do serve your long-term interests. On one hand, you can think of how to remove cues that lead you astray. On the other, you can reward yourself for behaviors that are consistent with your ultimate goal.

Arranging for something pleasurable immediately after you do something good will reinforce behaviors that will ultimately serve you well. Learning from your mistakes is beneficial, while tormenting yourself for them is definitely not. In fact, ruminating about your "weak character" or "lack of willpower" will deplete rather than increase self-control. Better to use it as an opportunity to study your pattern, act on your environment, and self-correct.

To take charge of what triggers and reinforces your actions, you need to become a good detective. You can do so by keeping track of what happens immediately before and after the behavior you want to change. The following exercise is a good start.

The behavior I want to change is:

_____

_____

Triggers: What is happening immediately before the problem behavior? Does it happen at a specific location or at a certain time of the day? Does it happen only in the presence of certain people? Do certain thoughts or feelings trigger the behavior?

_____

_____

_____

Action: What is happening as I perform this behavior? What am I feeling and thinking?

_____

_____

_____

Consequences: What happens after the behavior? What are the consequences? Are there certain rewards that maintain the behavior I want to change?

_____

_____

_____

How can I change the triggers and the rewards so that healthy habits will replace unhealthy ones?

_____

_____

_____

GREASE your plan

Thus far you have chosen a goal that is meaningful and important to you and identified one specific and measurable step you can take toward your goal. You have also considered obstacles that can get in your way and devised strategies to overcome them. Perhaps you have also kept track of a certain behavior you would like to change and identified what triggers you to engage in it and how it's reinforced. We would now like to offer you some additional strategies that will help you GREASE your plan:

1. Gradual: Take small steps, one at a time. Start with low-hanging fruit.
2. Rewarded: Praise and reward yourself for accomplishing small steps.
3. Easy: Make it simple for yourself so that you can experience success quickly.
4. Alternatives: Always have an alternative available: Fruit instead of a sugary snack?
5. Supported: Get your friends and relatives to help you and cheer you on.
6. Educated: Inform yourself. Don't eat just lettuce you proceed to drown with high-calorie Caesar dressing.

Make It Gradual

Take small steps at first and avoid shocking your system with drastic changes that are not sustainable. This is true for habits you want to reduce or eliminate, as well as those you want to begin or increase. Years ago we used to drink coffee with sugar: a flat teaspoon for me, two for Isaac. As we became more health conscious Isaac suggested we gradually reduce the amount of sugar in our coffee. Before long our coffee was completely sugar-free. Isaac stopped drinking coffee years ago, but I continue to enjoy it every morning, without sugar. I so enjoy my black coffee that I find it difficult to connect with its sugared and milky past.

Going cold turkey does work for some people; our son insists this strategy has been his path to a healthy lifestyle. When he decided to eliminate junk food from his diet he did it all at once, no exceptions; however, the milder, gradual approach is more sustainable for most people.

If your goal is to adopt a new habit, taking gradual baby steps will lead to higher self-efficacy and a greater likelihood of success. Self-efficacy is the belief you are capable of accomplishing what you set out for yourself.[27] High self-efficacy is associated with greater perseverance and a higher tolerance for frustration and setbacks. The more you experience success, the more confident you will become in your ability to accomplish your goal. Whether your goal involves getting up earlier in the morning, studying more, learning a new language, or exercising, it is best to start with baby steps you are more likely to achieve and can gradually increase.

For habits that are especially challenging for you, the steps may need to be particularly incremental. If exercising is a foreign concept that is difficult to institute, simply lacing your sneakers and going outside for a few minutes a day is a good start.[28] And remember the "if-then" strategy: "If I finished work for the day, I will put on my sneakers and go to the park across the street from the office before heading home."

Reward Yourself

If you are a parent of young children, reinforcing your kids for good behavior is very familiar to you. Whether it's a sticker for peeing in the potty or praise and attention for sharing a toy, you are well aware of the power of positive reinforcement. This is because providing immediate reinforcement serves to increase or strengthen a behavior. This is an overarching principle that works not only for children and not only for humans. But while we all dish out reinforcements, we are squeamish about reinforcing our own desired behaviors.[29]

If you think self-reward is silly, unnecessary, or exceedingly difficult to implement, think again. Individuals who are depressed are significantly less likely to reward themselves than those who are not,[30] and people who are successful in changing a targeted behavior are a lot more likely to self-reward than their less successful counterparts.[31]

The problem with most of our long-term goals is that the reward of better health, a higher grade, or paid debt is far in the future. It does not deliver the immediate gratification that can boost your self-change plans. When the dress hanging in the store calls your name, it's difficult to forgo buying it even if your ultimate goal is to save money. Having a new dress is immediately rewarding, whereas a savings account builds over time. You will enjoy the new dress now, whereas reaping the benefits of your savings is far less immediate.

In his best-selling book *Predictably Irrational*,[32] Dan Arieli recounts his experience of overcoming a serious illness that required him to self-administer nasty injections with exceedingly unpleasant side effects. For a period of months, this experimental treatment regimen consisted of three self-injections a week, followed by many hours of nausea, vomiting, fever, and other flu-like symptoms. Strict adherence to the injection schedule ultimately resulted in the sought-after cure.

Arieli later learned he was the only participant in this experimental treatment who was fully compliant with the punishing protocol. How did he do it? You may be surprised that it was not the prospect of a cure that sustained him throughout that period. Arieli had a routine that he followed every injection day. Being the movie lover that he is, he would pop in a DVD (or perhaps it was VHS at the time) of a movie he wanted to see immediately after he injected himself with the nasty medicine. He would then make himself comfortable and watch the movie. He began enjoying the movie immediately after injecting himself but before the harsh side effects kicked in. He also limited movie watching to injection days. Arieli believes he learned to associate the injection with an intriguing film and was thus able to stick with this punishing treatment regimen. Being disease-free was the ultimate goal and the greatest reward, but the movies sustained him throughout the difficult process.

You can think of self-reward as a bridge to your long-term goal.[33] It takes a potent arsenal to compete with the chocolate-glazed doughnut, the pretty dress, or the TV remote control. The small rewards you deliver along the way can hold you over until you experience the ultimate reward. The potency of immediate reward is due to its proximity to the behavior it is intended to reinforce. When it is delivered immediately and is contingent on the target behavior, it will serve to reinforce it.

In other words, two conditions must be met for a reward to be effective. It must immediately follow the behavior it is designed to reinforce, and it must be delivered only if and when the behavior takes place. Of course, one person's reward can be another's punishment, so make sure you choose something that is personally rewarding to you. It can be a tasty treat (providing your plan is unrelated to food), small purchase, or fun activity.

Back in the day of music CDs, a friend of mine would drop a dollar coin into an empty peanut jar every time he returned from his morning jog. When he accumulated enough for a CD or two, Jack would celebrate with a trip to his favorite music store. Eventually jogging became a habit—and an enjoyable one at that. Pretty soon, the high resulting from the release of endorphins, along with improved stamina, obviated the need for the coin jar.

Even a small reward, for example, watching a favorite show or calling a friend, can do the trick, so long as you do it immediately and only if you perform your target behavior.[34] A leisurely bath only if you exercise for twenty minutes; your favorite show only once you complete two hours of studying; a stroll on the beach with Isaac only after I finish this section of the chapter.

Complementing yourself for sticking with your plan is also effective. I tend to give myself a hard time when I am less productive than I would like to be. Thus, I find it very rewarding to savor the progress I'm making on an important project. Feeling productive is very rewarding for me.

Self-reward comes in many forms. A year ago, we took out a large loan for a small condo we purchased in East Harlem. Our son and daughter-in-law live there, and this has significantly improved the quality of their life. Knowing that they no longer need to move from one tiny and cockroach-infested apartment to the next is very rewarding for us. Nonetheless, the debt needs to be paid, and every month there is an automatic transfer of money toward the debt.

In addition, every few months when we have enough saved up, Isaac transfers more money than the minimum to pay the debt. He finds it extremely rewarding to see the shrinking debt and anticipates the next time he will be able to shrink it even further.

Which rewards work for you? How can you reinforce yourself for making progress toward your goal?

Make It Easy

Making it easy does not mean you should only set goals that are a cinch to accomplish. In fact, the best goals are ones that are important to you—achievable but optimally challenging.[35] Provided that it's achievable, you can definitely set a challenging goal, but you need to make it easy for yourself to make progress, especially in the beginning.

You don't want to become discouraged by making your first steps overly ambitious and then failing to meet them. I usually find I underestimate how long it will take me to complete a writing project. I now try to take this into consideration and thus avoid becoming dispirited. I set modest subgoals because I prefer to underpromise and overdeliver even if it is only to myself.

There are many things you can do to make it easier for yourself to act in the service of your goal. Limiting food intake to the dining room table can help you avoid mindless eating.[36] Clearing your house of junk food and replacing it with tasty but wholesome snacks can help you improve your diet. I once had a client who could not bring herself to throw away junk food altogether. Instead, she relocated it to the glove compartment of her car.

When Sandra would experience a strong craving she could not satisfy with a healthier alternative, she would have to make her way to her car to retrieve a treat. Simply erecting this barrier between herself and the coveted junk food helped her resist on many occasions. Sandra made it easier for herself to improve her diet by making it harder to indulge her unhealthy habit.

We have adopted a habit that Isaac has humorously named "prebeaning," inspired by, but diametrically opposite to, prepartying, a term we learned from our students. Unlike prepartying, where drinking begins well in advance of the party, prebeaning prevents us from eating unhealthy hors d'oeuvres at various functions we have to attend. We eat a healthy portion of beans, which we love, before we leave the house. This makes it much easier at the event to politely turn away from the appealing platters offered by the waiters.

Default payments and transfers to a savings account make it easier to save, while closing Facebook can make it easier to study. When I worked at a university counseling center I had a number of clients who struggled to keep up with their work. One in particular found that once he left campus for the day, his chance of studying diminished significantly. Kevin would go home, turn on the TV, and rarely hit the books. When he managed to take himself to the library after class instead of heading home, it was much easier for him to get his work done. We ultimately came up with a plan Kevin thought he was likely to implement.

On Mondays, Wednesdays, and Fridays, he was done with all his classes by 3 p.m. Organic chemistry was his last class for the day. Kevin made a rule that he would go to the library immediately after his organic chemistry class. If organic chemistry was over, it was time to go to the library. We did not specify how long he needed to stay in the library, only that he needed to go, sit down, and take out his books. Studying for even ten minutes would be considered mission accomplished. As you may have guessed, beginning his study session was the most difficult part, and Kevin soon managed to increase his study sessions and improve his grades. It was far easier for Kevin to get himself to study once he was at the library than to struggle with himself throughout the evening once he got home.

What can you do to make it easier for yourself to meet your goal? What small steps can you take to be successful and build self-efficacy? Which cues in your environment do you need to change?

Explore Alternatives

Without alternatives it is supremely difficult to renounce bad habits. If you're accustomed to something sweet in the middle of the afternoon to pick you up, don't give up on something sweet. You can replace candy with fresh fruit or an attractive fruit salad that you prepare in advance. I love crunchy food, and for a while I munched on pita chips whenever I craved a crunchy snack. It was certainly healthier than potato chips, I reasoned, which made it harder to eliminate it from my diet.

At a certain point I decided to replace pita chips with something healthier. I began with whole grain crackers and eventually "graduated" to either lightly salted brown rice cakes or spoon size shredded wheat with some nuts. I know it sounds ridiculous that plain rice cakes and shredded wheat can count as a satisfying crunchy snack, but believe me that for me they usually do the trick.

Finding alternatives is not just about nutrition. If you find yourself wasting your evenings in front of the TV, you can come up with alternatives. You may be so tired by the end of the day that mindless channel surfing is what you gravitate to. Think of a healthy alternative to being a couch potato that you can engage in at the end of the day. Perhaps shifting your exercise routine to the evening hours will work for you. It may give you the boost of energy you need to carry you through the evening.

If reading is something you would like to do more of, find an engaging but light read that can capture your interest even when you are tired. You are probably not in shape for a deep philosophical reading but may be game for something light and humorous. The point is to come up with an alternative to the behavior you want to change. We are always doing something, and the best way to deal with a problem behavior is to do something else instead. Choose a healthy alternative to your problem behavior and reward yourself for engaging in it.[37]

What are some alternatives that can help you achieve your goal?

Seek Support

Did you know that you are a lot more likely to smoke if you have a direct relationship with someone who smokes? Or that you are a lot more likely to be significantly overweight if your friends are?[38] If you are trying to lose weight, are you better off doing it on your own, in a group of people you don't know, or with your friends?

Other people influence us for good and bad. We like to think we make decisions independently of what other people think or how they perceive us. If you think so, you are wrong. We are wired for connection and pay close attention to what others think, say, and do. The closer those people are to us, the more they impact our decisions and behaviors.

If you're trying to change a problem behavior or adopt a healthy behavior, pay attention to your social circle. Try to surround yourself with individuals who engage in the behaviors you would like to adopt. Include those close to you in your change plan. Many students have told me that having a gym buddy helps them exercise on a regular basis. Even if they don't feel like getting up in the morning to go to the gym, they get up because they have made a commitment that they need to keep. It's a lot easier to stick to a healthy diet when others in your family share your goal and eating habits.

In some cases, those in your social circle may not share or even support your wellness goal. If you want to reduce your consumption of alcohol, your drinking buddies may try to dissuade you or even complain that you're no longer any fun. If your goal is to eliminate junk food from your diet, some friends and family may be inconvenienced or even threatened by your new lifestyle. Even a decision to learn a new language or write a book may be a source for concern to significant others, who may worry you will be too busy to spend time with them.

It's worth considering how you can include significant others in your change plan. Assure them your new interest is not a replacement for them. Avoid, at least for now, those in whose presence you are bound to engage in problem behavior.

On the positive side (and there is a lot more positive), other people can be a tremendous source of encouragement and support for the behavior you're trying to adopt. Compliments, encouragement, and support from those who matter most to you can help sustain your effort. When the going gets tough, as it often does, having loving and supportive cheerleaders can go a long way. The closer the cheerleaders are to you, the more important the role they can play in your change effort.

Support can come in many forms, from verbal encouragement, to hugs and high fives, to fun activities, to tangible rewards. I'm reminded of a former client in the final stages of his doctoral dissertation who hit an all-time academic dry spell. For various reasons, he found it exceedingly difficult to make any progress; his Ph.D. committee was growing impatient.

He attributed his ultimate success to his girlfriend, who planned fun dates but made them contingent on predetermined progress. Together they agreed on what he would have to "show" to be rewarded with an uber-fun date. The girlfriend did not wrest control or take charge of his goal, but she did provide an important incentive and made it conditional on progress.

In addition to celebrating your gains and cheering you onward, close others can help you through rough patches you are likely to encounter. Alcoholics Anonymous teaches those in recovery to reach out to their support person (sponsor) when they are about to engage in their addictive habit. Having such a person can, at times, help you overcome a strong urge to binge on junk food, go on a spending spree, or play video games for hours at a time. If you do slide back to problem behavior, close others can help you pick yourself up, dust yourself off, and get back on track. Gently reminding you of your goal or diplomatically alerting you when your behavior is inconsistent with it may be what you need.

At times, the best help someone can give you is not to get in the way of your goal. Ask others not to test your willpower by tempting you with a scrumptious pie if you are on a diet. Ask them not to pressure you to go clubbing if you want to stop drinking. If you have a tight deadline and need to work uninterrupted, ask your office friends to leave you alone for a while. Rather than enticing you with coffee breaks and lunch out, they can bring you coffee or lunch and ask what they can do to support you.

Support is invaluable and comes in many forms. Nonetheless, it is up to you to choose your support crew and let them know what you need from each one. It is generally good practice to complement generously, critique sparingly, and almost never nag.

If your behavior needs correcting, timing is of the essence, as is the manner in which such correcting is done. In other words, naysayers and naggers should not be recruited to your change effort. At the same time, it is up to you to not only tell your supporters what you need, but also give them feedback along the way. Don't expect others to read your mind and let them know what is working and what is not. In addition, don't shoot the messenger with annoyed responses to feedback you requested. [39]

Educate Yourself

A few months ago, I was Skyping with my older brother, who lives in Israel. Although he was slim and fit as a young man, as a sixty-plus-year-old he carries a few extra pounds, and his cholesterol and blood glucose are higher than they should be. We are close, and based on conversations with him and my sister-in-law, I'm aware of his sweet tooth and struggle with food. I suggested getting rid of sweets, but his youngest son, who at the time we spoke still lived at home, was not keen on the idea of a treat-free kitchen.

My nephew enjoyed treats here and there but did not have his father's high cholesterol nor his problem with self-regulation. At some point in our conversation, my brother insisted that high cholesterol runs in our family and there's not much he can do about it. Don't I remember how my mother struggled with high cholesterol despite her relatively healthy diet?

Whereas you may have a propensity for high cholesterol, high blood pressure, or depression, this certainly doesn't mean your future is predetermined and there is nothing you can do to prevent it. In addition, don't stick your head in the sand or pick and choose stories that support what you want to believe. My brother, by the way, also "reminded" me that our maternal grandfather lived to the ripe old age of 93, despite consuming three eggs a day. The point is you can find stories to support whatever you want, and some of them will be true.

We have a ninety-plus-year-old neighbor who is as sharp as a pin, still plays the fiddle in a quartette, and appears to be in excellent health. I asked her one day what is her secret. How does she do it? Knowing our interest in nutrition, Deedle, who plays the fiddle, was quick to respond with a naughty smile and a sparkle in her eye: "I do it by eating all the wrong things, my dear!" My witty and fortunate neighbor notwithstanding, I hope you don't need convincing that eating all the wrong things is not your route to health and longevity.

So, go to credible sources, read up, ask the right questions of the right people, and educate yourself. I've had issues with attention and focus my entire life. When I was an undergraduate student I was convinced that procrastinating on an assignment or waiting for the last minute to study for a test motivates me to buckle down. I pulled a number of all-nighters, which did little for my stress level, even if the outcome was not disastrous. I'm glad to say I educated myself about both the drawbacks of procrastination and healthier ways of dealing with attention problems.

No less important than information about your specific area of change is an understanding of what gets in the way of self-control. Guess what happened when McDonald's added healthier items to their menu? The sale of Big Macs went up! If you are scratching your head right about now, that's perfectly understandable. Was the taste of the healthier items so off-putting that customers immediately went back to their beloved Big Mac? Or did they simply worry that McDonald's is becoming so health-conscious that the Big Mac will disappear altogether?

Kelly McGonigal, Stanford psychologist and best-selling author of *The Willpower Instinct*,[40] has a more plausible explanation based on the psychology of human behavior. The option to choose healthy items fills us with optimism regarding our future behavior. We are so enamored with the healthy choices we will make tomorrow, or the next day, that this gives us a license to indulge today.

The principle of *letting tomorrow license today* is not only applicable to the decisions we make about food intake. We can easily convince ourselves that tomorrow or next week, we will be more motivated to finish that report, have more time to exercise, or be in a better position to save. In fact, in varied ways and across multiple domains, we can be surprisingly clueless about how our future self will behave. The one constant is that this future self will be more industrious, motivated, virtuous, and well organized. And you can definitely agree to give that keynote address in Timbuktu since it's two years away and you will surely have more time then. (Yes, Isaac, this one is meant for you.)

Knowing your less-than-stellar ability to predict your own future behavior can be an important tool in self-management. More options and greater choice will not necessarily serve your long-term interests.

You may be better off with the mean professor and her strict deadlines, or the gym membership that will not refund your money if you change your mind within the next 30 days. A savings account with stiff penalties for withdrawing money prior to a certain date may serve you well in more ways than one. Such accounts not only typically accrue a higher interest, allowing you to grow your nest egg, but also restrict your ability to make impulsive decisions you may later regret. This is a form of precommitment,[41] which you can use to your benefit, even without the rigid professor or the terms of the membership contract you cannot change.

If you know you have an issue with self-control in a specific domain, remember time alone will not change that, and your future self is unlikely to be in an infinitely better position to overcome it. Rather, think about what you can do to help yourself do what is needed for your long-term goal. A friend, who struggled with making good on her commitment to edit a book, gave a trusted friend a $500 check. It came with strict instructions to refuse to return all the money until the project was completed. Each of the first nine chapters was awarded with a $25 check; the remaining amount was returned when all 10 chapters were completed.

Remember, also, the tendency to be overly optimistic and fail to consider obstacles that can thwart your plan. Bringing such obstacles to mind can help you come up with a plan to overcome them. If I get a text message when I'm trying to study, I'll ignore it until I'm done. If my friend invites me to go to the mall with him, I'll suggest going for a bike ride instead. If I smell pizza in the staff room, I'll eat my lunch in my office.

Issues with self-control also explain why we often falter, despite our initial enthusiasm and confidence that we'll adhere to our plan. The reality is that setbacks are normal, and slipping up is not the exception but the rule.[42] Even those who are ultimately successful in achieving their goal and maintaining it throughout time rarely do so without bumps along the way.

Given that progress is rarely linear, do not get deflated and give up, or fall prey to the *what the hell effect*[43]—thinking that you can never do this and may as well throw in the towel. Just remember that self-management is a process that happens throughout time, and you are accumulating tools that can help you in the process.

On a personal note, a short time ago I got off the phone with my brother in Israel. A few minutes into the call, Hanan said, "Oh, by the way, I deserve kudos." He proceeded to tell me he had lost some fifteen pounds in the past few months and was feeling healthier and more energetic. He has never been one to exercise regularly, but he does go for long walks at least three times a week.

He did it by using a combination of strategies covered in this chapter. He got a lot of support from his wonderful wife, found alternatives to sweets, and rewarded himself for small gains. He even prompted me that kudos are in order—a great strategy for garnering support. Most importantly, they completely cleared the house of sweets once their youngest son left home for college. Maintaining this behavior throughout time is the next challenge, but one step at a time.

THE LAUGHING SIDE

You've been working hard learning about setting goals and creating positive habits. You've earned some comic relief. Let's say you want to improve your health—specifically, you want to lose weight. (We will get to regularity soon, don't worry. I know that's the real reason why you bought this book.) To lose weight you're going to have to change your behavior. I (Isaac) know it sucks, but I'm here to help you.

Before we begin, let's dispel a myth: Cold turkey strategies usually don't work. Let's dispel a second myth: If you have enough willpower you can do anything. Seven millennia of evidence show that human beings do not have enough willpower to even reach for the remote control.

The best we can do is to have a behavior change plan consisting of well-informed, achievable, small goals you can track and feel good about. The well-informed part is crucial because so many people give up bread for salads but shower their vegetables with enough dressing to fill a pool. Aim for slightly smaller portions. Find alternatives to lard that do not derive from animals fed toxins or exposed to environmental, bacterial, or fungal contaminants; mycotoxins, aflatoxins, ochratoxins, or gossypol (disclaimer: not a Gallup Poll subsidiary); and, my favorite, crotalaria.

I know the aforementioned list contains many threats, but you don't have to memorize it. You can cut and paste it into your smartphone's notepad. Every time you go shopping you can ask the guy lining up the tomatoes in the produce section to find organic foods free of environmental, bacterial, or fungal contaminants, as well as mycotoxins, aflatoxins, ochratoxins, phomopsin, sporidesmin, and spermicides. He will be more than happy to escort you to the nearest sanatorium, where you won't have to worry about any of this.

People think that without alternatives they will be able to overcome cravings. Impossible! Look at me. I replaced chocolate with such delicacies as carob-coated rye crackers that taste like UPS packing cardboard. I also replaced meat with a chewy substance that resembles regurgitated fungus. Instead of coffee, I drink chicory. For energy, I take a B-12 pill. For fun, I eat shredded wheat. And when I go completely crazy, I pour agave on tempeh and decorate it with wheat grass and sauerkraut. You see, there are alternatives. Granted it takes time and creativity, but if you go to the nearest health food store, you will meet a lot of friendly people who used to live a reclusive existence and are dying to help you.

What have we learned so far? Human beings have zero willpower. To overcome the tendency to traffic in clichés, you have to find alternatives to your terrible diet. These are behaviors you can learn. You don't need to wait until you have an epiphany, or colon problems, whichever comes first. You can make small changes to your diet, find suitable alternatives (carrot sticks instead of salami?), avoid depriving yourself, keep track of your slimming waist line, avoid second servings by putting a nice serving on your plate only once, tell a friend to help you by going to restaurants with healthy options, and, if you have bariatric surgery, within three hours you can completely forget about this nonsense.

Change: Pros and Cons

This book is all about change, but if you're really serious about it, you have to question the essence of change, the reason for change, and the pros and cons of change. Do not jump into it without an examination of pros and cons. This is hard, given the constant calls for change. *Adapt or die. Change or vanish. Adjust or bust.* Exhortations to change are everywhere, from political campaigns to organizational restructuring to therapy sessions. *To stay competitive*, we are told, *we must embrace change. The only constant is change. Change is an imperative.* But wait a minute, mister! Hold it right there! Who gets to decide what change is good for us? Is it the liberal media? The professorial elite? Chris Brown? Donald Trump? The Dalai Lama? Kellyanne Conway? Anthony Weiner?

Obviously, this is a topic of heated debate, but after years pondering this existential question I found the answer. To be honest, I (Isaac) found the answer when I was eight years old but waited fifty years to make sure I got it right. Now, at the ripe age of fifty-eight, I'm ready to share with you the authority on change. I looked high and low. I read extensively. I travelled the world. But at the end of the day, I found the answer close to home. The global authority on change is none other than yours truly.

This did not come easy to me, however. I've struggled with humility for many years, but I finally decided it would not be fair to deprive the rest of you from my transcendental revelations. The reason I'm the authority on change is because I've struggled with it my entire life. But after an inner journey, I decided that instead of me adjusting to the world, the world should adjust to me. I have empirical evidence to support my case:

1. *Thermostats*: Based on fifty-eight years of experience I discovered that the best temperature for me at night is 76.5° Fahrenheit—76° is too cold, and 77° is too hot—but commercial thermostats do not have a setting for 76.5°. To reach the desired temperature, I sleep half the night with the thermostat set at 76° and the other half at 77°. It is the only way to reach 76.5°.
2. *Underwear*: I find that 99% of all underwear brands in the world are either too tight or too loose for my physique. Just like thermostats do not have middle numbers, underwear do not have half-sizes. I know that I'm not the only person suffering from this type of discrimination, but I am the only one with guts to admit it. In a couple of weeks I'm going to Italy for work and am very excited to buy Intimissimi underwear, which is not available in the United States of Consumerism!
3. *Chairs*: Like underwear, 99% of dining chairs are not made for humans. Recently my wife and I embarked on a shopping expedition to replace our dining table and chairs, which had been damaged by a contractor who came to fix one thing and ruined seven others along the way. Shopping in this country should be easy, you think, until you rest your back on chairs with straight wooden backs made for Guantanamo. No wonder 90% of Americans suffer from back pain. Should I adjust to this crazy world, or should the world adjust to me, I ask.
4. *Sofas*: Our lovely contractor managed to ruin our sofa as well. After eleven excursions to Crate & Barrel, Macy's, JC Penney, Rooms to Go, IKEA, Robb & Stucky, Ethan Allen, and El Dorado, I found it inexplicable that most sofas would be either too high, too deep, or too low for my build. Again, no half sizes. Your knees dangle in the air because the sofa is too high, or your butt is so far back that the cushion ends at your heels, causing deep vein thrombosis (not to be confused with Trumposis, which is set to replace the zika virus as the most virulent epidemic affecting this country in centuries).

Our first trip to El Dorado lasted three hours. Ora, who thanks to extensive internet research knew more about the store than the salesperson, subjected the guy to interrogations about colors, makes, fabrics, prices, and country of origin the way custom officials interrogate refugees from Syria. I felt so bad for him that at the end of our visit I gave him $20. He looked puzzled, but I felt bad about leaving the store without buying anything. After all, these guys live on commission, and I have to live with my conscience.

5. *Self-deprecation*: Today you cannot even engage in self-denigration. As soon as you get started a few voices come from the woodwork to tell you that it is not good for you. Since when did self-dejection become so objectionable? Even social scientists tell you that self-deprecating humor is not good for you. Excuse me, but what if I'm perfectly happy with my defects?

It takes a lifetime to nurture a neurotic personality, and to give up on it to adjust to the world would be tantamount to treason. I choose authenticity, and you should too. Be brave. Hold on to your hard-earned neurosis, and, above all, do not replace it with Trumposis.

Happier, Healthier, Wealthier, Sexier

Becoming happy, healthy, wealthy, and sexy are goals many people share. I would have said universal goals, but a chorus of culturally sensitive colleagues would have challenged my imperialistic notions. So, let's just say a lot of people want to be happy, healthy, wealthy, and sexy, like the 7 billion inhabitants of the earth, minus my anticolonial friends.

To meet your objectives, whatever they are, you have to set goals, and not just any goals, but, as we have seen, SMART goals: Specific, Measurable, Attainable, Relevant, and Time-Bound. This is probably the single acronym in the entire book I did not come up with, but I have to admit it's pretty useful. Unachievable lofty goals—vegan restaurants in Newport News, Miami drivers signaling before they make a turn—can be frustrating.

A more specific and achievable goal would be to eat well every night. This is within my control, as I can eat *before* I go out to dinner. I can enjoy my delicious split pea soup at home before I go somewhere with a dubious record of catering to vegans. This goal is both specific and measurable. I can eat well every night: I can prebean. As Ora noted earlier, this is not different from what some young people do before they go out. They predrink, I prebean. It is also relevant because I don't like going hungry, and it is time-bound because I can implement this strategy right away and not in some distant future.

I have to admit I do pretty well at being happy and healthy, but I fail miserably at being sexy (in the narrow sense of sexy). This is because my health goals are incompatible with my sexy goals. After trying to build muscle for the last twenty years—organically, without the triple S (supplements, steroids, or soy)—I've decided to give up on that goal, which brings me to an important lesson: Perhaps your goal should be to change your goal.

In my case, despite a disciplined and highly neurotic exercise regimen, muscle-building is not in the cards for me. It is not an achievable goal, so instead of banging my head against the wall, I reframed my goal: Instead of being sexy I choose to be stylish. Being stylish is within my control: expensive Tumi bags, slim-fit suits, and ties that match my graying hair with my plain-looking brown eyes.

Being trim is also stylish, if you know how to dress—something that eluded me until recently. For the longest time I used to wear khakis that made me look like a clown, until one day I discovered slim-fit suits, pants, and shirts. All of a sudden, instead of a fool, I looked like a stylish stick. If you're going to give up on being sexy, as I did, it helps having a spouse who loves you unconditionally and thinks you're cute.

People think that if you have willpower you don't need any of these silly strategies. These are the same people who struggle with weight, addictions, cardiovascular disease, stress, lousy relationships, DUIs, debt, and psychopathy.

If You Can Do It, You Can Overdo It

Throughout my life I (Isaac) learned that if doing something is good, overdoing it must be wonderful. If gaining control is a good thing, gaining complete control must guarantee neurotic bliss. Welcome to my world. While my pursuit of goals and positive habits is admittedly a little rigid, it is informed by research. If you take the research minus the rigidity, you can learn something useful about changing your life.

The first driver of change is behaviors. Behaviors are things we do. As we saw earlier, to help us change we can work with behaviors in two ways: 1) set a goal, and 2) create positive habits. If you want to improve your well-being, you're going to have to change some of your behaviors by setting goals and creating positive habits.

You will have to work on eliminating some negative habits, for example, picking your nose in public, smelling your armpit as you walk down the street, and eating with your mouth open. When somebody objects to your point of view you get flustered, crawl into a fetal position, and call your *abuelita*. You'll have to change that, too.

Most of us do annoying things automatically, and they don't just annoy others—they have terrible consequences for us as well. For example, at the end of a perfectly good and satisfying meal you ingest five bowls of ice cream with six spoons of chocolate fudge amounting to 7,000 calories.

You walk into a movie cinema. As a zombie you buy the largest bucket of popcorn with extra butter. To flush it down you buy the largest soda. You eat it because it's there, not because you need it.

If you've ever tried to talk someone into healthier eating habits, as has happened to me, your companion usually tells you right off the bat that there is no point in giving up meat. Why, you naively ask, to which he replies that his great uncle had a cousin who had a friend who ate only caribou meat while he was wounded in Siberia in World War II and lived to be 107.

Sometimes, it's not just individual people who get defensive about eating habits, but entire cities. I recently was invited to give a keynote address at a conference in Sheffield, England. Everyone was exceedingly nice. I had a good feeling about this trip, until I tried to get a bite to eat. I admit vegans like me can be a pain in the butt to accommodate. Guilty as charged. But, you would imagine that an entire city would have some veggie-friendly eateries. This is what the locals thought anyway.

After a long search, I finally stumbled upon an Italian restaurant that advertised pasta fagioli, a traditional Italian soup. Feeling extremely self-conscious I awkwardly asked if the soup was mainly pasta or whether there were also beans. I know fagioli means beans in Italian, but I've had traumatic experiences before where I was served only constipating white pasta, so I wanted to be sure. I was reassured. Beans are one of my favorite foods: protein, fiber, and iron. What could be better? I was going to have a green salad with pasta fagioli.

After I ate a horribly overpriced beet salad with one leaf of lettuce and one thin slice of beet, I was anxious to get to my pasta fagioli. I was willing to put up with some white pasta for the beans. My soup finally arrived in a gigantic bowl the size of Texas, only a tenth of which had soup. I started eating, eager to chew on some beans. My fear increased the deeper I got into the soup. I was already three quarters into it, and I had yet to encounter a single bean. I knew fagioli was the plural of fagiole, which meant that there had to be at least two in my soup. I kept eating until I found one, single, lonely bean at the bottom of the soup. I was willing to risk some white pasta for the reward of some beans, but not just for *one*.

When I shared this with my hosts, not the entire bean experience—I was way too self-conscious for that—but that I couldn't find a veggie-friendly restaurant, they were very defensive and told me in unison that there is a lovely café behind the cathedral that opens between 10 and 10:20 a.m., every other day, in spring, where sometimes they serve brown rice. Wow, thank you! I wish I had known that ahead of time so that I could plan my trip—and bowel movements—accordingly.

Chapter Three

Emotions

THE LEARNING SIDE

Emotions, both positive and negative, are a part of life. We all experience them, to a greater or lesser degree, and you'd be hard-pressed to find anyone who prefers to be in a negative rather than a positive emotional state. Some people experience negative emotions more frequently and with greater intensity than positive ones. Others experience more positivity than negativity and typically feel upbeat and optimistic.

Whereas life circumstances can have an impact on our emotional state of mind, there is ample evidence that genes play an important role in where we reside along the happiness continuum.[1] Some of us are hardwired to experience more positive than negative emotions and vice a versa.

Genes and life circumstances notwithstanding, there is a lot you can do to experience greater happiness, satisfaction, and meaning in your life. In addition, you can become more skilled in identifying and managing negative emotions rather than getting caught up in them and behaving in ways that are self-defeating in the long run.

This chapter focuses on two important skills intricately related to well-being: how to create positive emotions and enhance life satisfaction and how to become more skilled in managing negative emotions. Remember that no matter where you are along the happiness continuum, there is a lot you can do to become happier and more fulfilled. You can't change your genes, but you can definitely take steps to improve the quality of your emotional life. Greater positivity is not only a lot more fun, but also associated with significant benefits to your health, career, and relationship with others. We will first focus on cultivating positive emotions and then turn our attention to managing negative emotions.

Cultivate Positive Emotions

Along with life and liberty, the pursuit of happiness is in the U.S. Declaration of Independence as a right to which all human beings are entitled. If you ask parents what they most want for their children, they will likely say first and foremost, they want their children to be healthy and happy.

As adults, we strive to lead a satisfying and fulfilling life with a lot more positive emotions than negative ones, even though we know we can't be happy all the time and are bound to experience our share of setbacks and heartaches. It turns out that what feels good to us is also good for us when it comes to happiness and life satisfaction. Positive emotions are not only important for the enjoyment of life, but also good for our health, relationships, ability to achieve important goals, and resilience in the face of challenges.[2]

Why Happiness Is Important

A psychological study on the lives of Catholic nuns provides a compelling argument for the relationship between positivity and health.[3] In the early 1990s, some 600 elderly nuns who took their vows as young women six decades earlier agreed to participate in a study on aging and Alzheimer's. They agreed to be followed up on a regular basis, have their past and present records explored, and ultimately donate their brains to research post mortem. In the course of the study, researchers stumbled upon a gold mine of data they had not initially anticipated.

Prior to taking their final vows and beginning their work in the community, the young nuns were asked to write a short essay about their life and their decision to become a nun and enter the convent. These essays were discovered years later when these women were quite elderly and some had already passed away. The essays, written by these women in their youth, were analyzed for the level of happiness and positivity contained in them. The number of words and sentences containing positive emotions were independently coded by researchers, who had no knowledge of how long these women lived. Each essay was then assigned to one of four quartiles ranging from the least happy to the most happy.

Even if this is the first time you're hearing about the nun study, you may already be guessing what the data revealed. Indeed, there was a strong association between the level of positive emotion expressed in the essays and how long these women lived. The median age of death was 86.6 for those classified as least happy and 93.5 for those classified as most happy—a difference of 6.9 years. Remember that happiness in this case was inferred from a single essay written 60 years earlier.

The study is not without limitations, as noted by the researchers and common to most studies. For example, most of the essays were largely positive, even those in the least happy group. It is quite possible that these young women were aware that the essays they wrote could influence their career paths, not unlike essays submitted as part of the college application process. It is also possible that they were in a particularly exciting phase of life, and this served to inflate the level of positivity expressed in the essays. Nonetheless, this research is in line with other studies that point to the strong association between positive emotion and life expectancy.[4]

In addition to longevity, positive emotions are linked to other health benefits, for example, an improved ability to recover from the common cold and a lesser likelihood of contracting it,[5] a lower rate of cardiovascular disease, and quicker recovery following injury.[6] This is largely due to the fact that positive emotions can undo the corrosive impact of chronic negative emotions on our health and wellness. And if positive emotions are good for physical health, they are an integral part of social, psychological, and occupational well-being.

According to the broaden-and-build theory,[7] positive emotions can also broaden our perspective and help us consider different paths toward achieving goals and resolving difficulties. Think about the last time you experienced an intense negative emotion like extreme anger or fear. What did you think about at that time? Chances are you could think of little else aside from the person, situation, or circumstance at the center of this emotion. Being hyperfocused on one thing is adaptive if you need to flee a dangerous situation; however, this narrow and constricted thinking will not serve you well in most cases.

Whereas negative emotions lead to narrow and self-focused thinking, positive emotions can broaden and expand your perspective. When you feel upbeat and positive you are more likely to see possibilities and potential solutions, and think in more creative and innovative ways. When faced with challenges, you're more likely to generate different courses of action, evaluate the pros and cons of each one, and take active steps to resolve the problem.

Being proactive increases self-efficacy[8]—the confidence in your ability to overcome obstacles and achieve important goals. Positive emotions facilitate adaptive coping, and this further contributes to positive emotions.[9]

Positive emotions toward others lead you to seek connections and invest in relationships. Since it's more pleasant and rewarding to spend time with people who are cheerful and optimistic, positivity helps build social capital. This, in turn, contributes to your happiness and ability to thrive. Happiness facilitates relationships, and good relationships result in more happiness. Positivity is also associated with generosity and kindness toward others. You are more likely to be attuned to the needs of others and willing to lend a helping hand when you are in a positive mood. You can think of positive emotions as fuel for developing your resources—intellectual, psychological, and social resources.[10]

Pleasure, as Well as Purpose

You want to have fun, experience pleasure, and be happy. At the same time, you will probably agree that there's more to life than simply being happy. Consider that researchers in the nun study found that despite differences in happiness demonstrated in the essays, all of them were largely positive. In fact, the initial plan to also identify negative emotion in those essays was abandoned given that negativity was in short supply. What do you make of this? Is it no more than a calculated attempt on the part of the young nuns to come across as positive? We think not.

By definition, nuns are religious and have a strong faith in God. Belief in a greater power outside oneself can provide a sense of coherence and direction to one's life. Religion plays an important role in the lives of many people. It provides them with answers to some of life's most perplexing questions and is a source of comfort and personal identity.[11]

Being part of a congregation can also provide social support and a sense of belonging. While religion isn't for everyone, it does confer a certain benefit as far as happiness and well-being are concerned. Many people report feeling spiritual or otherwise connected to something larger than themselves, even if they are not drawn to organized religion or have any religious inclinations whatsoever.

In addition to their religiosity, the young nuns probably had a strong network of support, a sense of community, and a belief that they were making the world a better place. These are key ingredients for psychological well-being. Helping other people and working for causes that one believes in benefits those on the giving end as much, if not more, than those on the receiving end. Well-being is about not only joy and enjoyment, but also engagement, personal growth, and the pursuit of meaning.[12]

Some things we do strictly for pleasure even if they do not provide us with meaning or purpose. Other things are worthy and meaningful to us even if pursuing them is hard and not always enjoyable. Parenting young children, for example, is something many people find deeply meaningful and rewarding but also limiting and not always purely enjoyable.

Investing in a challenging project that requires sustained effort during a long period of time is another example. The process can be grueling at times, but you stick with it because you have a goal you want to reach. We need pleasure, as well as purpose, and finding the right balance between the two is crucial.[13]

What about you?

What makes your life pleasant and enjoyable? List two to five things and explain how they contribute to your happiness.

1. _____

2. _____

3. _____

4. _____

5. _____

What makes your life meaningful? List two to five things and explain how they contribute to your well-being.
1. _____

2. _____

3. _____

4. _____

5. _____

How do these lists compare? Is there any overlap between what makes you happy and what makes your life meaningful?[14]

Cultivate Positive Emotions

It is probably not news to you that the incidence of depression has grown throughout the years and is the cause of suffering and reduced productivity for scores of individuals. Depression plagues many people and is often referred to as the common cold of mental health. Despite this, most people are not depressed and report being at least moderately satisfied with their lives. We seem to have a hardwired tendency to perceive even neutral events as slightly positive, a tendency that probably contributed to our species' long-term survival.[15]

While most people do not struggle with depression, they do not necessarily function at their best and lead a rich and meaningful life. Flourishing is about being at our best and achieving excellence in important domains of life. People who flourish are highly engaged with their families, careers, and communities. They set meaningful goals and work hard to achieve them.

According to research by Barbara Fredrickson,[16] the balance between positive and negative emotions needs to be skewed toward positivity for flourishing to occur. It's not that negative emotions can or should be eliminated altogether, but they should have a much smaller footprint in our lives. We tend to pay a lot more attention to negative information and consequently need to balance that with far greater positivity.

The good news is that we can take active steps to not only manage and reduce negative emotions, but also increase and amplify positive ones. So even if you are not a born optimist who tends to see the glass as half full, there is a lot you can do to increase your well-being and become happier and more fulfilled. The field of positive psychology has made a strong case that alleviating suffering is not enough.

Many people who are not struggling can nonetheless benefit from expanding their well-being toolbox. The strategies you are learning about in this book are designed to do just that. Next, we expand on strategies that have been thoroughly researched and found to help many people. You will probably find that you gravitate more toward some strategies than others. You are the expert on yourself, so pick those that appeal to you and try them out.

Build on Your Strengths

Focusing on strengths—yours and those of others—is far more powerful and beneficial than focusing on weaknesses.[17] It is also a lot more pleasant and rewarding. Parents and teachers do this when they focus attention on children when they are at their best and behaving in productive and desirable ways. Savvy managers do this when they allow employees to do what they do best and acknowledge their contributions. Identifying and amplifying strengths is consistently associated with higher levels of happiness, lower levels of depression,[18] increased productivity, and superior performance.[19]

This is not to say there is no place for acknowledging weaknesses and working to remedy them; however, rectifying weaknesses without amplifying strengths is of limited value. Unfortunately, this was the modus operandi for many years in education, industry, and psychology.

A few months ago, at a psychology conference, I (Ora) bumped into a former supervisor from my early days as a school psychologist. As we caught up during dinner, I told him I would likely cringe now at some of the psychological reports I wrote early in my career. This is because my training at the time was largely focused on diagnosing learning and behavioral disorders, and coming up with intervention plans. Little, if any, time was spent on spotting and building on strengths.

When I think back to my own schooling as a child, I can recall few instances where strengths were celebrated or even acknowledged. Perhaps this is one reason why many of us are uncomfortable talking about what we are good at or proud of ourselves for. Doing so may seem immodest, self-indulgent, or both. If this hang-up applies to you, we suggest you shelve it for the time being and consider the following strength-based exercises.

1. Think about a situation where you were at your best or felt most proud of yourself. Describe this situation in detail. What did you say or do? Who else was there? What impact did this have for you or someone else? What makes this situation stand out for you?

_____

_____

_____

_____

2. Make a list of your positive traits and qualities. List no less than five positive traits you possess. Then write about how these positive qualities manifest in your life. Are any of them underused? What can you do to put them to good use?

_____

_____

_____

_____

_____

3. As you focus on your strengths and positive qualities, consider new ways you can use them in your life. How can you build on these strengths and/or apply them to different domains of life? Other than yourself, who else may benefit by you using your strengths in different ways?

_____

_____

_____

_____

_____

4. What can get in the way of you using your strengths? How can you tackle such obstacles?

_____

_____

_____

_____

_____

5. Think about a person(s) or even a pet(s) that is important to you. Now consider the ways you are important to them and enrich their lives.

_____

_____

6. How do you think others perceive your strengths? What would those who know you say are your strengths and best qualities? How, from those people's perspectives, can you further build on your strengths or apply them to other domains of life?

7. What in your life are you energized and excited about? What do you most look forward to? How does this pertain to your strengths?

8. Are there any strengths that are misused or overused? If so, which strengths do you need to dial back[20] and how?

9. Are there any strengths you know you possess but are reluctant to use? What are those strengths and what is the source of your reluctance? What can you do about that?

10. What strengths you would like to develop that you consider realistic and within your control? What do you need to do to develop them? What would you gain from developing these strengths? What can get in the way and how can you address potential obstacles?

Adopt an Attitude of Gratitude

Isaac recently spent a week in Naples, Italy, presenting at a conference and running a two-day workshop. He has been studying Italian for many years and saw this as an opportunity to practice the language, while making a contribution to the profession. When the invitation to present initially arrived, we considered what to do.

For me, staying home alone for a week is not an option. I have a form of muscular dystrophy and require some assistance at home. I've also had some nasty falls, making it unsafe and impractical to be alone for extended periods of time. Isaac suggested that I join him, but I decided it was not worth the effort, given that he would be busy teaching most of the time. I receive some paid assistance on a daily basis but did not particularly feel like having someone stay with me on a full-time basis for a week; however, I was prepared to do so since I wanted Isaac to enjoy himself in Italy without having to worry about me.

This is where gratitude comes in. Rather than spending a less-than-ideal week with a paid assistant, I had a magnificent week with my amazing sister-in-law, Myriam, and incredible niece, Yael, both of whom traveled from Israel to stay with me. As if the stars aligned, it turned out to be a perfect time for my sister-in-law to take time off from work and for my niece, who was between semesters.

Airline tickets were particularly inexpensive, as it fell between the high-season summer months and the Jewish new year. We spent the week recounting family stories; engaging in deep, meaningful conversations; and laughing ourselves silly. We went for long strolls on the Hollywood boardwalk, right next to our condo. On three occasions, we went out early enough to see the sun rising over the ocean. We shopped until we dropped, given the easy access to Aventura Mall and the bargain prices for them.

As the week drew to an end, we decided to make this special girls' weekend a new family tradition we will continue to uphold. Amid stories and laughter, we expressed our gratitude for the close relationship we have and the special time we were sharing. I was (and still am) incredibly grateful they chose to come. I know how busy they are and how difficult it is to get away. They, in turn, said this visit was an incredible gift to them as well.

There is substantial evidence that an attitude of gratitude is good for your health, relationships, and overall well-being. It is also associated with greater empathy, forgiveness, and kindness toward others.[21] Such simple practices as keeping a gratitude journal or counting one's blessings have been found to have a significant and lasting impact on life satisfaction. In a seminal study, one group was asked to keep a gratitude journal while another group was asked to list daily hassles. A third group received no intervention whatsoever. Compared to the other two groups, those who kept a gratitude journal were more hopeful and energetic. They also exercised more and reported fewer physical symptoms.[22]

Another well-known gratitude intervention demonstrated the benefits of writing a gratitude letter to someone you have not properly thanked for what he or she has done for you.[23] Writing such a letter can give you a happiness boost, especially if you follow that up with a gratitude visit where you deliver the letter in person. And you can probably imagine how good it feels to be the recipient of such a letter and read about how much you have benefited someone you care about. The following exercises are designed to help you foster an attitude of gratitude:

1. Make a habit of taking a few minutes each day to think about the things in your life you are grateful for. Your list can include big things like good health and close relationships. It can also include mundane things like the sight of a pretty rainbow or a pleasant walk in the park. Making a list of five things you are grateful for that day can boost your spirits. If keeping a written list is not a good fit for you, make a mental list of blessings using the fingers of one hand to keep count.
2. Choose one day during the week to think about and list your blessings for that week. Some researchers have found that doing this once a week can have a more powerful impact than a daily list of blessings, which can become mundane.[24] Others prefer to do this on a daily basis, so try it out to see what works for you.
3. Think about a person in your life who has done much for you and had a decidedly positive impact on your life. Dedicate thirty minutes to writing a letter expressing your gratitude to this person. Provide detail on what this person has done for you and what the impact has been. If it feels right to do so, make time to visit this person and deliver your letter. Once you have done so, write about the experience of writing and delivering the letter.

Relish and Savor

"Life is what happens to you while you're busy making other plans." This beautiful piece of wisdom can be found in "Beautiful Boy," a song John Lennon wrote for his beloved son Sean. Another quote from the song speaks to Lennon's excited anticipation of watching his son grow up: "I can hardly wait to see you come of age."

John Lennon was tragically killed that same year, on December 8, 1980, at the age of 40. Sean was five years old at the time. Father and son, both born on October 9, thirty-five years apart, celebrated their last birthday together that year. The fact that John Lennon did not live to see his son grow up gives special meaning to the reminder that, "Life is what happens to you while you're busy making other plans."

Life is both precious and fragile, and there are no guarantees that any of us will live to a ripe old age. This is why the ability to be present-focused and savor life's beautiful moments is so important. Although we are all well aware of the finiteness of life, we often fail to take time to relish our experiences. Time spent making plans for the future or recounting past events can come at the expense of attending to and savoring the present moment.

Furthermore, future-oriented or past-oriented thinking can detract from happiness when it involves worrying about the former or regretting aspects of the latter. When our minds are not where we are but somewhere else, we are not fully inhabiting or enjoying our experience. I often think about this when I see couples or groups of friends, each fully engrossed in their smartphones. I think about it even more when I see young parents sitting with their children at a restaurant but attending mostly to their devices.

Conveniently, the children, some barely toddlers, have their own devices to keep them entertained. My own son, who turns thirty in a few months, is married and living in New York City. What I would give today to relive those moments from his early years. We have a wonderful relationship today and many fond memories, but I'm sure I did not fully appreciate the finiteness and preciousness of those early years.

We cultivate positive emotions when we attend to positive experiences and the enjoyment we derive from them. This may be more evident when you're sitting on a park bench on a beautiful spring day during your lunch break; however, even such mundane activities as your morning shower or first cup of coffee can be made more enjoyable by attending to its pleasurable aspects. Savoring is anything that can extend and intensify the enjoyment of your experience.[25]

It's amazing how totally unnoticeable or thoroughly enjoyable a cup of coffee can be, depending on whether you mindlessly gulp it down on your way out the door or take time to enjoy its rich fragrance and deep flavor. Even brushing your teeth or washing the dishes can be pleasing when we mindfully attend to these tasks. On the flip side, what once inspired and amazed us can become mundane if we let it. We adapt to most things, good and bad, and the happiness we derive from a beautiful new home or even the beauty of nature can fade and diminish throughout time.[26]

When we first moved to Miami eleven years ago, we lived in a small apartment on campus while we looked for a house. I was completely captivated by the beautiful Coral Gable campus—the beautiful, ancient trees and well-maintained green space, and Lake Osceola with its turtles and jumping fish, pelicans, ibises, and other birds. My all-time favorite was the resident crocodile, which could be spotted floating in the lake or sunbathing by its edge, jaws wide open. I felt a thrill whenever I spotted the huge, dinosaur-like reptile, whom I nicknamed "Shmulik" (a Hebrew nickname for Samuel). With time, the initial awe faded, and what was once striking became mundane and frequently overlooked. I would often rush to meetings and classes, mentally reviewing my long to-do list, almost oblivious of my spectacular surrounding.

My fascination with my crocodilian friend was the exception, as spotting it would always give me a high. Sadly, the crocodile was the victim of a greedy hunter and is no longer there— another reminder that nothing lasts forever.

My awareness of the downside of adaptation led to increased efforts to pay attention to diverse aspects of this beauty and feel grateful for having this in my backyard. Research studies support the notion that varied experiences are less prone to hedonic adaptation than static ones and that adaptation can be further thwarted by having an attitude of gratitude.[27]

We ultimately bought a home directly across the street from campus, which means I can get there in three minutes with my wheelchair. This not only enabled me to continue working once I was no longer able to drive, but also means I'm still able to remain engaged in campus life, as well as continue to enjoy its natural beauty now that I can no longer work. I often think about the richness this adds to my life and feel grateful to be in this privileged situation. I'm well aware that most people with my level of impairment do not have such easy access to such a valuable resource.

What about you? What can you do to keep experiences fresh and engaging? What are you grateful for and how can you maintain this attitude of gratitude?

We can do much to relish and savor the present, as well as positively anticipate future events and recall memorable and meaningful ones from the past. Isaac and I often reminisce about how our son's passion for chess was sparked some twenty-two years ago, when an ad in our local paper caught my eye. Matan was eight years old at the time, and we were living in Kitchener, Ontario. The ad was for a weekly chess class in the neighboring town of Guelph.

We somehow thought this would be a good fit for Matan and enrolled him in this class. It was a forty-minute drive on back roads, longer during the winter months, when black ice has to be factored into the mix. Isaac and I would take turns driving Matan to this class. I remember working on my doctoral dissertation at a local coffee shop as I would wait for Matan to finish his ninety-minute class.

On the drive back home, he would excitedly share what he had learned. This began Matan's love affair with chess. He competed in tournaments in our town and elsewhere. Chess really became "his thing" and continues to be a source of growth and meaning. These days Matan is a popular chess coach in New York City and is nurturing the next generation of chess players.

Anticipation of future events can also guide our actions and the goals we set.[28] For example, planning a vacation in Italy can fuel an interest to learn Italian and motivate you to enroll in a class. Joining a book club can enrich your social life and also motivate you to read more. As you become absorbed in a book, you may also anticipate the engaging discussion that will follow at the next book club meeting.

If you enjoy a weekly date night with your partner, you can get creative in planning an "out of the box" experience your partner is not expecting but will enjoy nonetheless. It doesn't have to be anything lavish or spectacular, but surprise, variety, and creativity can add an extra special spice to the experience. You can then anticipate the event, relish the experience, and reminisce about it in the future. The following activities can also help you focus on positive anticipation and reminiscing:

1. Write about a peak experience you have had in the past few months. What made it so special? What does it say about you and what does it mean for your life?

2. Think about an upcoming event you are looking forward to. Describe it in detail, including where you will be, what you will be doing, and who you will be with. Write about your anticipation of this event and/or share it with someone who is likely to share your joy.

_____

_____

_____

_____

_____

Find the Silver Lining

Twenty years ago, my brother Hanan had a freak accident. He was a successful dentist in Israel and the sole wage earner in his family of six. His wife was a stay-at-home mom at the time, and his four children ranged from five to fourteen years of age. One day his car broke down, and he hopped on a city bus. When he got off at his stop, he failed to notice the partially melted ice cream cone someone had left on the step.

My brother slipped and tumbled to the street, dangerously close to the rear wheels of the bus. The bus driver was oblivious to the entire incident. Thinking his passenger had fully disembarked, the driver pulled out from the station and ran over my brother's right hand. That incident changed the lives of my brother, his wife, and their four children.

The fact that he even survived is miraculous given the massive amount of blood he lost. Survive he did, but his right hand was severely and irreparably damaged. His career as a dentist was over. He underwent surgery and intense physiotherapy, but the only outcome was considerable and persistent pain he lives with to this day.

I'm sharing my brother's story with you as an example of one person's ability to find the silver lining. Despite the grave personal, familial, and economic consequences of this accident, my brother did his best to cope. His tendency to look at the bright side of things served him well as he struggled with the accident and its aftermath.

A few years ago when we spoke on the phone, he said something that exemplifies his outlook. He recounted how busy he had been building his clinic and his career while his two older sons were growing up. He would often come home at night when the boys were already in bed. He was a dedicated father and did the best he could, but there was simply too little time. It was different with his two younger children, who were eight and five at the time of the accident. Unable to work and undergoing various treatments, time was one commodity he now had in ample supply. Being able to spend more time with his children and strengthen the bond was my brother's silver lining. If gratitude and savoring is about noticing the good in the good, silver lining refers to finding the good in the bad.[29]

The field of positive psychology has highlighted the human capacity to cope and even thrive in the face of adversity and challenge. Terms like posttraumatic growth[30] and benefit finding[31] have been used to describe this remarkable capacity.

Calamity has many forms: grave illness, serious loss, death of a loved one, and more. These are things we pray will never happen to us or those we love. Nonetheless, such things do happen, and some people are incredibly resilient in the face of such challenges. Whereas they would not choose these experiences, they point to positive growth and change that ensued as a result. Becoming more resourceful, kind, and sensitive to human suffering are some of the noted benefits, along with an increased ability to attend to life's beautiful moments and let go of minor hassles and grievances.

On a lighter note, finding the silver lining need not only apply to serious illnesses or life-changing freak accidents. Isaac and I recently had a four-day mini vacation in Orlando. In a completely uncharacteristic fashion, we accepted an irresistible vacation offer in exchange for attending a ninety-minute interview with a timeshare agent. We made the commitment in a moment of weakness but had neither the time nor the will to follow through with it when the time came. Nonetheless, we packed our bags and headed to Orlando for four days. We thought this would be an opportunity to check out Disney World, which so many people rave about. Big mistake!

The annoying timeshare interview was a lot less aversive than visiting the Magic Kingdom. The huge crowds, long lines, and artificial surrounding was definitely not our cup of tea. After forty-five minutes, Isaac became totally claustrophobic and begged me to leave. It was clearly a waste of time and money (yes, we still paid for Disney World), but we got plenty of laughs from the experience, mostly at ourselves.

We also laughed about some of the characters we encountered and the unskilled agent who behaved like a bad car salesman. We also listened to audiotapes of engaging lectures and excellent fiction, and enjoyed spending time together. We lost time and money but found the silver lining.

Manage Negative Emotions

When I was a nineteen-year-old undergraduate student, my boyfriend of more than a year ended our relationship and broke my heart. It was my first serious relationship, and as far as I was concerned the breakup happened out of the blue. I was deeply attached to not only my then boyfriend, but also his parents and two siblings, who welcomed me into their family.

My own parents were living overseas at the time. It was the final week of classes, and finals were looming large. There were papers to be written and finals to study for. Yet, I was feeling lonely, rejected, and sad—not the greatest mindset for academic success.

If this story piques your interest, it's not because it's exotic (it's not), unusual, or profound. Throughout the years, first as a mental health professional and later as a professor, I've encountered many students with similar variations of this story. Rather, it is the shared human experience of loss and pain, and how these emotions are managed, that makes this story relatable. For me, the experience of my heartbreak (yes, it really felt like that at the time) and how I coped with it (stay tuned) were highly formative in my own development as an emerging adult.

Healthy and Unhealthy Ways of Managing Emotions

People manage their emotions in different ways. Some ways of managing negative emotions are healthy and adaptive. They are adaptive because they help us deal with distressing emotions in a manner that promotes rather than harms our well-being. They enable us to deal with our pain in a way that is consistent with our values, goals, and relationships.

Unfortunately, people do not always manage their emotions in a healthy and constructive manner that serves them in the long run. They engage in behaviors that help them feel better in the short term but impede their long-term health and happiness.

Back to the story of my breakup. Before I share with you how I coped with this adversity, I would like you to consider the opposite of healthy coping. What are some maladaptive ways of managing negative emotions in general and this scenario, in particular? List at least five unhealthy ways of coping with this situation. Provide a rationale for why you believe these ways of coping are unhealthy and/or unhelpful.

Unhealthy responses to the breakup scenario:

    1. _____.

       This is unhealthy because _____.

    2. _____.

       This is unhealthy because _____.

    3. _____.

       This is unhealthy because _____.

    4. _____.

       This is unhealthy because _____.

    5. _____.

       This is unhealthy because _____.

I assume that some of the following have made it to your list:

- using drugs, alcohol, or food to blunt negative emotions
- isolating yourself from others
- brooding about the possible causes and consequences of the breakup
- blaming yourself
- coming to the conclusion you are a failure in relationships
- perceiving yourself as unlovable
- neglecting responsibilities (in this case, not working on papers or studying for exams)
- seeking revenge
- ignoring your feelings altogether and/or denying that you are having a difficult time
- comparing yourself to the people you know who are happily attached and thinking how much better off they are in comparison to you
- eating unhealthy food and neglecting to exercise

In the throes of emotional upheaval, some people resort to such strategies, even though they know they do not serve them well. I am proud to report that my response to the breakup was considerably more adaptive. The first thing I did was look for my best friend to share the news with her. I remember how we both skipped class, opting instead to sit on the grass and have a heart-to-heart talk. She was empathic and supportive, while also expressing confidence in my ability to get through this.

Once the initial shock had subsided, I made a resolution to not allow this to get in the way of my studies. As a psychology major I knew I could not ignore my feelings or deny my pain. I decided to schedule regular study sessions, in addition to a designated time of day when I could attend to my feelings. When I would catch myself thinking about the breakup in the midst of a study session, I would remind myself that I have allotted a special time for such thoughts. I also reminded myself of my long-term goal of getting into graduate school and my resolution that this would not interfere with my studies.

I sought support from close friends, completed my work, and got involved in a drama club, where, incidentally, Isaac and I met thirty-five years ago. Life certainly unfolds in mysterious ways. Okay, to be perfectly honest, my determination to come out on top (I'll show him! This won't break me! He'll regret this!) did provide some of the fuel that facilitated my coping. I'm only human.

When life throws you a curveball and you encounter a difficult situation, how do you respond? Do you typically respond in a manner that protects your health and your most cherished relationships and aspirations? Do you sometimes do things that are ultimately unhelpful even though they provide a short-term reprieve from pain? Is your response appropriate for the situation you are in? In this case at least, my response to this curveball was highly adaptive. I cannot claim, however, that I always employ the best strategies in all contexts. After all, life is a work in progress, and we are continuously learning and adapting.

This section provides an opportunity to consider the strategies you use to manage unpleasant, painful, or distressing emotions. I encourage you to reflect on what you do and how it is working for you. Examining your strategy toolbox can help you consider those you want to build on, as well as those you are better off without. In addition, there may be strategies that are currently not in your toolbox but you may want to learn and implement.

According to a wise proverb often attributed to famous psychologist Abraham Maslow, "When all you have is a hammer, everything looks like a nail." This is what it's like when you have limited tools at your disposal for managing difficult emotions. You use the same tool, even though it's ineffective or not appropriate for the particular context you find yourself in. Greater awareness and a willingness to examine and update your toolbox can enhance your ability to manage negative emotions in a constructive manner and improve life satisfaction and well-being.

Understand Your Emotions

Intelligence is not just about verbal fluency and the ability to think abstractly and solve complex problems. The burgeoning field of social and emotional intelligence has highlighted the importance of accurately perceiving our emotional experience and responding to emotions, especially negative ones, in a thoughtful and constructive manner.[32] Of course, this is easier said than done, especially in the midst of an intensely unpleasant emotional experience. This is when people are most at risk for impulsive, maladaptive, or even destructive behavior.

The more we understand and accept our emotional experience, the better off we are. This includes an awareness of what triggered a particular negative emotion; what thoughts, sensations, and behaviors are associated with it; and what response is most appropriate in this situation. If you have a diffuse negative emotion but cannot pinpoint what you are actually feeling, you are not in a good position to take constructive action.

People who are adept at differentiating negative emotions have a wider repertoire of strategies for managing their emotions and are less likely to feel overwhelmed by them than their less emotionally savvy counterparts. Consequently, they are less likely to respond aggressively, drink excessively, or resort to other counterproductive means of soothing their emotions.[33]

It is important to remember that negative emotions are an inevitable part of being human and a normal response to life's challenges. They are adaptive when they are in proportion to the situation and lead us to constructive action. For example, feeling bad because you hurt someone's feelings can motivate you to apologize. This is providing you are able to accurately interpret your feeling as remorse, own up to the fact that you have hurt someone, and apologize for your behavior.

However, negative emotions can also intensify and escalate like a tornado. Many of us have had the experience of saying or doing things we later regret. This is usually when we are in the throes of extreme negative emotion. This is because rampant negative emotions can hijack our brain and interfere with rational problem-solving.

When we are aware of our emotions and understand how they affect us, we are more likely to be able to manage them. Conversely, being disconnected and out of tune with our emotional experience may result in an excessive response that is disproportionate to the situation at hand. If you are unaware of your "hot buttons," you may find yourself reacting in ways that are perplexing and even troubling to yourself and those around you.

The following exercise is intended to help you monitor the interaction between your thoughts, feelings, and behaviors in a given situation.

Reflect on a recent situation where you experienced negative emotion:

Context: What was the situation? Where and when did it take place? Who were you with?

_____

_____

_____

Thoughts: What was going through your mind? What were you saying to yourself? Which images or pictures were playing in your head? How did you interpret this situation?

_____

_____

_____

Feelings: How did you feel? How did your thoughts, images, and interpretation of the situation affect your feelings?

_____

_____

_____

Physiology: What bodily reactions did you experience (i.e., increased heart rate, sweaty palms, butterflies, etc.)?

_____

Behaviors: What did you do? Did your behavior change during the course of the event? Do you think your behavior helped the situation or made it worse?

_____

_____

_____

How well do you think you handled this situation? What, if anything, could you do differently next time?

_____

_____

_____

You can become a good emotion detective by discovering the relationship between what you say to yourself in certain situations, how you feel, and how you respond. When you discover that your thoughts and behaviors are making the situation worse, you can take active steps to respond in a healthier, more productive manner.

Decide What to Feed

According to a Native American legend, a wise grandfather wanted to teach his grandson an important lesson about life. Said the grandfather, "Inside me there is a great fight between two wolves. One wolf is filled with anger, envy, sorrow, and regret. The other wolf is filled with love, joy, kindness, and hope. These two wolves are fighting inside of all of us, yourself included." The grandson thought for a few moments and then asked his grandfather, "Which wolf will win the fight?" The grandfather's reply was simple: "The one you feed is the one who wins."

This simple legend contains a powerful message about life in general and negative thoughts and emotions in particular. Rumination is the term used by researchers and clinicians to describe repetitive and incessant thinking about a negative event. People who ruminate replay negative events in their minds time and time again, recounting what happened, how it happened, and why it happened. While they may think this helps them understand the problem and can facilitate a positive outcome, this is rarely the case. Coupled with negative emotion, this type of thinking is often distorted and typically leads to spiraling into negativity.[34] Rumination, which is more common in women than men, is akin to feeding the angry, sorrowful, and revengeful wolf.

If you have a tendency to ruminate, there are strategies that can help you better manage it, if not overcome it altogether. Remember that the grandfather did not say that one must fight or kill the miserable wolf within. Refraining from feeding it is enough. In other words, you can recognize a ruminative cycle, acknowledge that you are caught up in it, and decide to refrain from feeding it any longer.

Remind yourself that rumination biases your perception of reality and impairs rather than facilitates problem-solving. Just because you think something doesn't make it true, even if your thoughts are quite convincing. Feeding the miserable wolf only feeds your own misery, so try starving it instead. You may not be able to totally eliminate these repetitive, maladaptive thoughts, but you can decide not to buy into them and take them as God-given truths.

Go for a jog, call a friend, or find another healthy distraction that can help you exit the downward spiral of rumination.[35] A ruminative cycle is like a tornado that gains force and intensifies. The earlier you seek refuge, the easier it will be to extract yourself from its aversive grip.[36] Tell yourself that you can solve this problem later when you are in a better state of mind for appraising the situation and taking constructive action.

In fact, rumination breeds pessimism and passivity, and is associated with a host of mental health problems. There is a healthy menu of adaptive strategies for managing distressing emotions, so try to pass on the ruminative junk food.

Practice Acceptance and Self-Compassion

There is a powerful relationship between what we say to ourselves, how we feel, and what we do. How you interpret a situation will affect how you feel about it. Your feelings will have an impact on the actions you take. The actions you take will then affect how you think and how you feel. As you can see, thoughts, feelings, and behaviors create a self-reinforcing loop.

Imagine that you have just helped yourself to a generous portion of chocolate cake even though you have been working to improve your diet. After you pop the final forkful of cake into your mouth, you begin to berate yourself for being so weak. You tell yourself that you have no self-control and will never manage to lose weight or change your eating habits. You feel sad, discouraged, and disappointed in yourself. What impact will this have on your self-control? Are you more or less likely to act constructively? It will probably come as no surprise that strong negative emotions can reduce self-control and lead you astray.[37] You may even be tempted to drown your sorrow with more cake.

The best you can do in such situations is to be forgiving and kind to yourself despite your transgression. You may think that "letting yourself off the hook" will make you weaker, but this is not what the research shows. In fact, treating yourself with compassion will make it more likely that you will act to ameliorate the situation rather than make it worse.[38]

Self-compassion involves three core components. The first component is to acknowledge your suffering and treat yourself kindly, even if your own behavior is the source of it. It is about accepting the fact you are not a perfect human being but deserve to be treated kindly and compassionately nonetheless. The second component is the understanding that none of us are perfect and all of us suffer at some point or another. Sometimes our suffering is due to external causes that are outside of our control, whereas at other times our own behavior is the source of our suffering.

Reminding ourselves that suffering is part of the human experience can be a source of comfort. We are not alone in our suffering, and we make mistakes, like everyone else. Being mindful of our own emotional experience is the third component of self-compassion. If you can mindfully attend to your painful experience and accept it, you are less likely to go down the rabbit hole of a self-reinforcing emotional tornado.[39]

Mindful approaches to managing negative emotions contain a simple yet powerful message: Negative thoughts and negative emotions can be accepted rather than feared, ignored, battled, or challenged. Oftentimes, actively trying to get rid of a certain thought or image (*do not* think of a pink elephant) makes it certain that we will be unable to do so. In fact, the harder we resist and fight, the more we fan the flame. There is a better way of dealing with such experiences that entails seeing them for what they are, as well as what they are not.

Accepting unpleasant or painful internal experiences without overidentifying with them can protect us from taking them too seriously and losing perspective. A dark cloud is more likely to pass if you are also aware of the sky. If your mind is the sky that is aware of the dark cloud, you are less likely to get lost inside that cloud.[40] It is better to accept the emotional dark cloud rather than try to suppress it or force it from the sky.

If you are confronted by an aggressor who intends to harm you, you need to act by either overcoming the aggressor or fleeing the situation. Our built-in "fight or flight" response enables us to protect ourselves by taking swift action. In general, our attempts to exercise control over our environment and the situations we encounter in our lives are adaptive and can serve us well; however, we run into problems when we attempt to control internal experiences in a similar manner. What applies to the external world outside the skin does not bode well for private experiences.[41] In fact, attempts to force ourselves to think or feel differently can be distressing in and of themselves.

Rather than trying to control what you think and feel, you can focus on what you do in the midst of emotional turmoil. Feeling angry is okay, lashing out at someone is not. Imagine that your sister-in-law made a snarky comment that made you angry. If you are in touch with your feelings you acknowledge to yourself that you are feeling angry. You also understand that you have a choice as to how to respond.

Depending on the context, you may choose to tell her you are upset, walk out of the room to cool off, or ignore her comment altogether. Remind yourself that negative emotions are a part of life, that they can be tolerated, and they don't last forever. Your own behavior is what you need to control.

Take Constructive Action

Taking constructive action is about doing something helpful or effective in a particular situation. When it comes to managing negative emotions, some ways of responding are never adaptive, as noted earlier. Lashing out in anger, drinking yourself to oblivion, or indiscriminately avoiding any situation that may be emotionally challenging are some examples. You may be surprised that maladaptive strategies are at times prescribed by ill-informed practitioners.

For example, some people think that punching a pillow while imagining that it represents the face of your foe is a good way of letting off steam. In fact, research has shown that blowing off steam in such a way will only make you angrier and less likely to respond in a constructive manner.[42] It is definitely better to deliver a punch to a pillow than to the face of a person you are upset with, but it is far better to avoid punching altogether.

We also know that using strategies as an escape from unpleasant emotions can come back to bite you. A person with social anxiety who worries about feeling awkward at a social gathering may decide to avoid the situation altogether. While this may feel good in the short term, you can probably see why it would not be adaptive in the long run. On the other hand, there are situations or even individuals that you are better off avoiding if engaging with them is consistently toxic for you and there is no good reason for doing so. In other words, context is everything.

Your best bet is to do an accurate assessment of your own emotional experience, as well as the situational demands. If you can clearly identify and label your emotion, and understand the thoughts, behaviors, sensations, and situations that trigger and maintain it, you are in a better position to do something effective and constructive. Problem-focused coping refers to behaviors designed to directly address and tackle a problem situation. While there are individual differences in people's problem-solving capacity, this capacity can be enhanced through training.[43]

The following template provides a systematic approach to solving problems:

1. Write a brief description of the problem you are faced with.

_____

_____

_____

_____

_____

2. How can you address this problem? Brainstorm possible courses of action.

_____

_____

_____

_____

_____

3. What are the pros and cons of each alternative?

_____

_____

_____

_____

_____

4. Based on your evaluation, what do you think is the best course of action? What specifically do you need to do to implement it?

A. What will you do?

B. How, where, and when will you do it?

C. What obstacles might get in the way? How can you overcome these obstacles?

_____

_____

_____

_____

_____

5. Did your plan work? Did it make the situation better? How so? Describe the positive change that resulted from your actions. If things did not improve, what do you need to do differently?

_____

_____

_____

_____

6. What have you learned from this process that can help you in the future?

_____

_____

_____

_____

These simple steps represent a systematic and effective way of responding to many life obstacles, from the mildly annoying, to the highly distressing, and everything in between. Changing what we do can result in a change in how we feel and think. Even though we can get worked up about certain situations, it's helpful to keep in mind that many problems can be resolved, and we can take steps to address them.

Being proactive can contribute to self-efficacy, the belief you can accomplish things and achieve goals despite barriers. If you are stressed about a work situation and understand what is fueling your stress, you can consider which strategy would be most effective in this situation. Should you get to work a bit earlier to give yourself more time? Do you need to delegate more rather than try to do it all yourself? Do you need to initiate a conversation with your supervisor, supervisee, or coworker, if that is the source of the problem? Are you appraising the situation accurately and constructively?

You can take steps to alleviate an already distressing situation, but you can also be proactive regarding an upcoming stressor. For example, if you have good reasons to believe your position is on the chopping board, you can update your resume and start to look around for a job that would be a good fit for your interests and skill set. In other cases, you may come to the conclusion that you are better off avoiding certain situations altogether.

A young woman I know developed significant mental health problems in response to a high-paced and stressful work environment. At one point, her anxiety skyrocketed out of control and she contemplated suicide. Thankfully, she received support from astute family and friends who understood the gravity of the situation and sought professional help. She ultimately realized that her job was a poor fit for her. She resigned and found one that was a much better fit for her personality, interests, and skill set. Simply changing jobs resulted in improved physical and emotional well-being.

Acting to solve problems works well when the issue at hand is something that is within your control; however, it is important to keep in mind that we sometimes face distressing situations due to circumstances that are beyond our control. These situations call for different strategies that also need to be in your strategy toolbox. You are probably familiar with the serenity prayer that is used in Alcoholics Anonymous and other twelve-step programs: "God, grant me the serenity to accept the things I cannot change. The courage to change the things I can. And the wisdom to know the difference."

I think there's a lot of wisdom contained in this simple statement, even if you choose to omit the reference to a higher power. We need to distinguish between situations we can change by directly acting on them from those we cannot change but need to live with, accept, and make the best of. Emotion-focused coping refers to such strategies, which focus on our emotional reactions to the distressing situation. Acknowledging our suffering, treating ourselves with kindness, and reaching out for support are healthy strategies for managing distressing situations that are beyond our control.

I end this chapter with yet another reference to the wise statement attributed to Abraham Maslow: "If all you have is a hammer, everything looks like a nail." Hopefully, this chapter has provided you with a menu of options for cultivating positive emotions and managing negative ones. The best we can do is have a range of strategies at our disposal and apply them according to what is a good fit for us and what the situation calls for.[44]

If we determine that a particular strategy did not work as well as we had hoped, we should be flexible enough to reverse course and try something else. Remember that life is a journey and a work in progress that inevitably entails bumps along the way. Negotiating the bumps is often difficult, but it can also be exhilarating and even life-changing. In the following chapter, we turn our attention to the role our attitudes and beliefs play in shaping our experience. As we will see, some situations are best tackled by addressing or even challenging our own internal dialogue. Along with problem-focused and emotion-focused coping, appraisal-focused coping can further expand our emotional toolbox.[45]

THE LAUGHING SIDE

To improve your emotional state you have to do two simple things: Reduce negative emotions and increase positive emotions. Mathematically speaking, this is expressed as follows: EWB = +E / -E ^%$#@, where "EWB" means emotional well-being, "+E" means positive emotions, "/" means over, "-E" means negative emotions, and "^%$#@" means ^%$#@.

Let's say your husband was nasty to you (he told you you spend too much money on plastic surgery—this is Miami, remember?) and that we assign this negative interaction a numerical value of –3. According to certain theories, the way to alleviate the negative feelings associated with this exchange is for your husband to suck up to you three to five times the value of the emotional wound he inflicted upon you (remember, it was –3); therefore, for hubby to come clean, and for you to feel good, he will have to come up with something positive in the range of +9 to +15 (3 x 3 equals 9; 3 x 5 equals 15). Once again, this is based on the theory that for each negative emotion you need three to five positive emotions to temper the impact of the pain he caused you.

At this point you open the internet, pull up your wish list from the Gucci store, and forward him the link as a hint of how he might redeem himself. There are lessons here for men and women.

Ladies:

1. Never have fewer than five items on your wish list.
2. Make sure the items on your wish list are at least five times the cost of your most recent plastic surgery.
3. Put the Gucci link in your favorites.

Gentlemen:

1. Compared to Gucci bags, your wife's plastic surgery is something you might actually enjoy.
2. ^%$#@.

Always look for opportunities to feel good, laugh, express gratitude, love unconditionally, forgive, and minimize negativity in your life. I know this sounds like commune talk from the 1960s, but it may actually do you some good, and if you're a man this may save you thousands of dollars.

Love Often, Laugh Often

Even ascetic people like me (Isaac) need positive emotions like joy, gratitude, pleasure, satisfaction, affection, love, intimacy, closeness, and *sex*. Positive emotions serve three very important roles in life: 1) They're good in their own right (warmth, laughter, affection, *sex*), 2) they're great buffers against negative emotions, like lack of *sex*, and 3) they expand our creativity and ability to solve problems.

This is how it works. In addition to enjoying the moment, collecting positive emotions is like building a personal bank of affirmative feelings. When I get a little depressed, I can draw on the bank of positive emotions to compensate for feeling blue. So, head over to your wife right now and give her a kiss, and a hug, and then go to your daughter's room and tell her how much you love her. Hopefully your wife and daughter will reciprocate, unless they think you're totally weird and ask you to throw this book in the incinerator.

To demonstrate this concept in a class I was teaching with Ora, after an argument between us in front of class I walked across the room and gave her five kisses. Remember, research says that for every negative interaction with your spouse you need five positive ones.

Your cells remember good times. The neurons you haven't destroyed with drugs in college store a lot of happy moments. When adversity descends upon you, your brain recalls positive emotions (like *sex*) to counteract negative experiences. Positive emotions are not only fun, but also they protect us against negative ones. They make us resilient.

But in addition, positive emotions make us more creative and intelligent. Research published in some prestigious journals by some prestigious people with incredibly prestigious resumes says that feeling happy makes you more resourceful. When you laugh you can see all kinds of connections—not just dealing with sex—that you cannot perceive otherwise.

There are multiple ways to experience positive emotions. Laughing is a great one. Hugging (not strangers) is another. Expressing gratitude is highly recommended. Helping people and showing them affection is awesome. Feeling proud for accomplishing a SMART goal is totally cool. Writing down things that are going well for you in life also produces happy hormones.

Make it a goal to laugh often. I intersperse my reading of serious stuff, like psychology or social issues, with humor. I know it sounds cliché, but I do subscribe to the *New Yorker* mainly for the cartoons (and the "Shouts and Murmurs" page, which keeps rejecting my submissions). I also subscribe to *Time*, mainly to read "The Awesome Column" by Joel Stein, whose humor I love. I also get the Borowitz Report delivered to my inbox to keep my sanity about politics. I tape the *Daily Show* for the same reason.

To survive Miami, I also read Carl Hiaasen, and no matter what I'm working on, I always get a dosage of Dave Barry and David Sedaris, along with Sam Levenson. I also would have said Woody Allen, but to like him is very politically incorrect. And no matter what kind of lousy day I had, an episode of the *Big Bang Theory* is always a great relief. Come to think of it, it is a complete miracle I have time to do anything else during the day.

Make it a goal to love often, too. Display warmth and affection. Be kind to others. Listen to them quietly. Do not interrupt. Ask open-ended questions that show others how much you care about them. If you're a jerk, it will feel a little strange at first, to you and to them, but after a while, it will become a positive habit, unless you're an incurable jerk.

There are a million ways to experience positive emotions: practicing your favorite musical instrument, reading an inspiring book, going for a walk, enjoying nature, meditating, playing sports, studying, having a great conversation, fantasizing that you're with Scarlett Johansson. Don't miss opportunities to collect positive emotions. They will come in handy when you're down in the dumps. But don't collect just happy emotions; you also need meaningful experiences, like helping humanity in some fashion, and for God's sake stop obsessing about *sex*.

WARNING: BIG WORDS AHEAD

Research says eudaimonic positive feelings are as important as hedonic ones, if you know what the heck they mean, of course. [46] Eudaimonic feelings have to do with thriving, flourishing, realizing your potential, growing as a person, making a contribution to the world, and finding meaning in life. Hedonic feelings, in turn, are momentary pleasures, like having an ice cream, or, well, ok, sex.

If you ask me, I would want a balanced portfolio, with a mix of both kinds. But if you're totally addicted to momentary pleasures, without any intention to grow as a person or find meaning, please tell me how to do it so I can stop feeling guilty.

Messianic Times

I waited for months. I read up on it. I cleared my calendar. I talked to my friends about it. I was ready. I actually became quite religious about the whole thing. I discovered things about myself I was never aware of. In fact, I turned into a fanatic, a true believer. I even bought a forty-six-inch TV for my exercise room, just to make sure I did not miss any of his appearances during my futile attempts to build muscle.

Messi was about to deliver spiritual redemption during the last World Cup. For us Argentinians, Messi was to bring salvation. We felt we scored with Pope Francis. It was now time for Messi to score. What could be better than the world talking about how great Argentinians are, instead of all the talk about defaulting on international obligations and government corruption?

I even thought of buying one of these ridiculously expensive Argentina shirts, which cost more than the forty-six-inch TV we impulsively acquired, but I resisted. Matan, our son, caved. After the first match Argentina won, he went to the closest Adidas store in New York City and dished out half of his teacher's salary. Although Matan was born in Canada and never lived in Argentina, he absorbed my irrational love of soccer. After leaving Argentina at the age of sixteen, encouraged by the fascist dictatorship, I renounced most Argentinian traditions, except soccer.

My productivity during the 2014 World Cup plummeted. Thank God it was during the summer, when the university slows down. Otherwise, I would have been fired. But truth be told, most of my colleagues did the same thing, running to meetings and finishing papers in between games. To make sure I did not miss any games, I blocked my outlook calendar with the relevant games and set up my DVR—successfully I might add—to record the games. My assistant knew not to schedule any meetings during the eighty-four matches.

During the final game against Germany, I was a nervous wreck. It was good Matan was here in Miami to debrief. He gave up playing in chess tournaments to come home and watch the last week of games with us. We're both equally irrational about soccer. When Higuaín scored during that game, the two of us jumped up and down like kangaroos. When the referee disallowed the goal, we were crushed. I used Spanish vocabulary unbecoming of a dean of education. Ora did her best to console us.

My behavior during the last game was consistent with the overall regression I was experiencing. For the entire World Cup, I went back to childhood, when my life revolved around soccer. During the tournament, I woke up thinking about soccer, spent hours watching reruns, and—something that did not exist when I was a kid—wasted valuable time following blogs. Matan, who is an elitist, insisted we follow the *Guardian*'s blog. But let's be honest, he is right. No American commentator really understands soccer.

On ESPN, we were served Alexi Lalas for breakfast, lunch, and dinner. Lalas used to be a decent soccer player, but he is highly irritating as a commentator. You see, we're not just any kind of soccer fans, we're soccer snobs. The only redeeming quality of Alexi Lalas is that he speaks English. To comment on the games, ESPN invited foreign players, mostly from Latin America, whose English did not bring much pride to their educational system.

Despite the terrible defeat in the final game, and the ensuing depression, which lasted several days, I benefited greatly from the World Cup. For once, I could speak authoritatively about sports in the United States. I could show off in front of colleagues. I could say things like, "The 4–4–2 formation is working defensively" and "Sabella needs to bring Gago to reinforce the midfield."

In addition to these displays of sublimated testosterone, my mental health also benefited greatly. Not since I was nine years old had I taken such complete leave of my senses. For four weeks, I showed complete disregard for work, responsibilities, and anything resembling mature behavior. That proved to be very therapeutic for a workaholic like me. I also gained a lot of sympathy from friends and colleagues who wanted Argentina to win, just to make me happy. Bonding with Matan over soccer, that was priceless.

Chapter Four

Thoughts

THE LEARNING SIDE

"Nothing is either good or bad, but thinking makes it so." Shakespeare wrote this in *Hamlet* more than four hundred years ago. Much earlier than that, Epictetus, a Greek-born slave who was eventually freed and became a great philosopher, said, "Men are disturbed not by things, but by the view which they take of them." There is no need to rigidly adopt this worldview that it's only thoughts that matter.

Many things, like oppression, child abuse, or extreme deprivation, among others, are bad and harmful in and of themselves. These things should disturb us and propel us to act to eradicate them. Nonetheless, these quotes make an important point about the powerful role thoughts play in shaping our experience.

Our mind is a meaning-making machine that is constantly appraising what we encounter. If you are faced with a challenging situation at work, you may feel excited, overwhelmed, or resentful based on how you assess this challenge and your ability to handle it. If you think it presents you with an opportunity to learn new skills, you will feel excited. If you think it exceeds your abilities, you will feel overwhelmed. If you think your boss unfairly dumped this in your lap, you will feel resentful. How you appraise the situation will affect your feelings and actions.

Surprisingly, we often fail to consider the powerful impact our thoughts play on how we feel and what we do, or don't do. We attribute our actions and emotions to external events without fully considering how our mind is making meaning of those events. At times, our appraisal of situations dampens our mood and reduces our inclination to take constructive action. If you think about it, thoughts do not directly cause you to do anything. In fact, thoughts cannot even "cause" emotional distress if we do not believe them or take them too seriously as literal truths. [1]

This chapter covers two important skills related to thoughts. The section entitled "Challenge Assumptions" is an overview of proven strategies for examining our thoughts and changing or better managing ones that keep us stuck. The "Write a New Story" section is about how we can transform our lives by taking action that is consistent with our values and advances our cherished goals.

Challenge Assumptions

Just as we are susceptible to doing things that may not serve us well or, in some cases, even harm us, our thinking patterns can take us down an undesirable path. For example, we experience stress when we encounter a situation and perceive that it can threaten our well-being in some manner. This applies to such tangible threats as a menacing-looking stray dog in our path or a suspicious sound in the middle of the night.

Our system then prepares us to act by going into a fight or flight mode. Our heart pumps blood at a faster rate, our pupils dilate to improve our visual acuity, and adrenaline flows through our veins and primes us for action. Whereas this can be lifesaving in the face of genuine threat, the same system also kicks into effect in situations where it is counterproductive to do so.[2]

Evolution, which equipped us for self-preservation, has not sufficiently fine-tuned our system to immediately differentiate between situations that pose a real threat versus those that do not. This is why a pounding heart or a pit in your stomach can appear when you get an e-mail that your boss wants to meet with you, during an argument with your partner, or upon finding out that your three closest friends got together without you.[3]

If you hear a suspicious noise during the night but quickly figure out it's your furnace, which is in need of servicing, you will feel an immediate sense of relief and your system will soon return to normal. This was a false alarm. But what if this is the first time you hear this strange noise? You will think you are at risk, but this thought is misleading, because you're not—it's just the furnace pounding. This is irritating but definitely not dangerous. You have made an erroneous attribution regarding the source of the noise. This misattribution is what fueled your anxiety.

Faulty appraisals can also be at play as we navigate our relationship with colleagues, friends, loved ones, and ourselves. What if your close friends are meeting to plan a surprise birthday party for you? Or if the reason your boss asked to meet with you is because she's impressed with your work and would like you to mentor junior colleagues? The point is that your feelings and actions can be based on faulty appraisals and misattributions. You can jump to unwarranted conclusions that fuel negative emotions and can lead to unconstructive behaviors.

Because we talk to ourselves all the time, we often don't realize what we are actually saying to ourselves and whether it is accurate or helpful to think this way. We believe that what our thoughts are telling us is an unvarnished reflection of reality. We don't stop to consider that the same situation can be interpreted in multiple ways, some more adaptive than others, and that how we feel and what we do next is based on the meaning we attribute to it.

This is because our thoughts are so automatic that we may not even be aware of what they are telling us. They are particularly susceptible to "slipping through," unnoticed and unexamined, when they accompany bad or anxious moods.[4]

I remember when I first learned this as an undergraduate student in the late 1970s. It was at the time that the cognitive revolution in psychology was gaining force, and Aaron Beck and Albert Ellis, a psychiatrist and psychologist, respectively, published their work on helping clients change maladaptive thinking patterns. I distinctly recall the "aha moment" as I sat in the large lecture hall, at the edge of my seat, listening to my professor. I was fascinated with what I was learning and began to examine my own thinking traps[5] and their impact on my moods and behaviors.

Thinking about my own thinking, and especially its vulnerability to errors and misjudgments, was meaningful from a personal and professional perspective. Years later I would detect similar "aha moments" in the faces of clients and even students as we covered this in counseling courses.

Learning to identify and evaluate negative thoughts can be a valuable addition to your well-being toolbox. You may well discover that what you're saying to yourself in stressful situations is only making matters worse. Keeping track of the thoughts that accompany negative emotions will enable you to scrutinize them for accuracy and utility. You may even discover predictable thinking patterns that fuel your distress but often operate below the radar. You can then explore if modifying a problematic thought or your relationship to this thought leads to improved moods and behaviors.

Understand and Detect Negative Thoughts

Isaac and I recently returned from a week-long Caribbean cruise. Unlike your typical cruise, this was a conference focused on the health benefits of a plant-based diet. We ate healthy and delicious vegan meals, listened to compelling lectures by world-class health experts, and connected with others who share our passion for healthy vegan food. The two of us also gave a talk on—you guessed it—well-being! Isaac covered the domains of well-being, while I presented on strategies for change.

If you are reading this book you already know Isaac is a comedian, in addition to a serious academic. He is in his element in front of large crowds and skillfully sprinkles informative presentations with (often impromptu) humor. He has given hundreds of invited talks throughout the years in various countries and continents. His is a difficult act to follow. I, on the other hand, am made from a different cloth. I believe I am a good teacher overall, and my talks throughout the years have been well received. Nonetheless, I do not possess Isaac's high self-confidence or his level of chutzpah and willingness to take risks and push the envelope.

I'm generally somewhat anxious prior to a public speaking event, as I was on the morning of our scheduled cruise presentation. It didn't help that we were the only speakers scheduled for that morning, which meant we had a large audience despite the 8:30 a.m. start. The larger the audience, the more pleased Isaac is, and the more nervous I feel.

Nonetheless, a minute before I took the microphone from Isaac to begin my talk, I decided to deviate from my plan. I opened by telling the audience that Isaac possesses all the humor in the family, so they shouldn't expect much. But, since I don't want them to think he's perfect, I shared with them what Isaac sheepishly confessed on our first morning of the cruise: He had forgotten to pack the charger to my laptop. I must have said this in a rather dramatic tone of voice, given the outburst of laughter in the room. I immediately felt the tension leaving my body.

I'm sharing this story because in addition to using it to alleviate my public speaking anxiety, I circled back to it when I talked about the power of automatic thoughts. As you can imagine, hearing that I have a laptop, sans charger, was unwelcomed news. I brought my laptop along for three main reasons. First, we had planned to do some work during the downtime when the cruise ship is at port and most people disembark for excursions. We know from experience that without taking a taxi, which I cannot do with a power wheelchair, there's little point in leaving the ship. Second, I typically make last-minute changes to my PowerPoint slides as I review them close to the time of the presentation. Third and most importantly, I was hoping to project the slides from my laptop and thus be able to view my notes as I presented.

Learning that my laptop charger was left at home was a clear inconvenience, and I was irritated. Such hassles are far from catastrophic, but they often lead to unpleasant moods. Nonetheless, the specific emotion, and its intensity, depends on the automatic thoughts that are swirling in our heads on such occasions. Imagine, for example, that I had the following thoughts:

- I reminded him to unplug the charger and put it in the case!
- I can't believe he forgot such an important thing!
- He wouldn't forget the charger to his own computer!!

Anger is the predominant emotion generated by such thoughts, and yes, I admit to feeling some anger. Now consider the emotion that would likely come in the wake of the following thoughts:

- OMG! Now I won't have access to my presenter notes!
- I can't make any changes to my presentation!
- There will be tons of people there, and I'll be really nervous!
- What if I don't do a good job? People will be sorry they came!
- It'll be terrible if it's not a stellar presentation—especially since I have to follow Isaac, who is such a great speaker!
- I won't be able to make progress on the book without the charger and I'm already behind schedule!

This type of thinking provokes anxiety. Of course, one can feel both angry and anxious, with each emotion reinforcing and perpetuating the other. Moreover, taking impulsive action based on such emotions further feeds into the negative thoughts–emotions–behaviors loop. I'm sure you can see why launching into a scolding and blaming diatribe would be counterproductive, even if it provides a temporary relief from pent-up tension. No, I did not do that.

Because we often fail to notice how negative thoughts feed aversive emotions and can lead to maladaptive responses, keeping a thought record can help illuminate this pattern. Table 4.1 can help you see the relationship between the situations you encounter, the emotions you feel, your thoughts, and your actions. [6]

Tracking the automatic thoughts that accompany stressful situations can be an eye-opener. Your thoughts, which often fly beneath the radar, can now be inspected and are no longer automatic. You may be surprised to know that while most of us experience intrusive negative

Table 4.1.   Anatomy of an event.

Situations	*Thoughts*	*Emotions*	*Actions*
What was going on? Where were you and with whom?	What thoughts or images were going through your head? How much did you believe each thought? (0-100%)	What emotions (sad, anxious, angry, etc.) did you experience? How intense was each emotion? (0-100%).	What did you do?

thoughts at one point or another,[7] there are good reasons why we should not take them at face value.

For one thing, these thoughts are often sneaky—they pop into our heads, uninvited, unannounced, and often unnoticed, hence their automatic quality. In addition, they masquerade as objective facts and seem highly plausible and convincing. In reality, such thoughts are often biased, inaccurate, or distorted. They are not necessarily altogether wrong, but they do not take all the facts into consideration.

Finally, automatic negative thoughts can make you feel bad and get in the way of taking constructive action. The antithesis of allowing thoughts to control your emotions and behaviors is to notice, examine, challenge, and change—either the thoughts themselves or how you relate to them.[8]

Challenge and Modify Negative Thoughts

Automatic negative thoughts appear factual to us, but this is not necessarily the case. As any sophisticated consumer of information knows, things we hear or read about can be true, partially true, or completely false.[9] This holds for our own thoughts as well. Yet, we rarely subject them to the same rigorous process we apply to information we consume. People who are depressed or struggle with another mental health issue are particularly susceptible to distorted, biased thinking. It's as if they have an invisible filter that screens out any information that is not consistent with their troubled mood.[10]

Thoughts that lead to strong negative emotions are prone to some of the following traps:

- Polarizing: Thinking about things in all or nothing terms. If something isn't perfect, it is worthless.
- Overgeneralizing: Thinking that one setback will affect every domain of life.
- Catastrophizing: Anticipating the worst possible outcome in a situation.
- Filtering: Seeing yourself and the world through a negative filter. Positive experiences are ignored since they do not fit with your negative filter.
- Labeling: Putting negative labels on yourself or others, rather than thinking that you or someone else made a mistake.
- Personalizing: Automatically thinking that others' negative behaviors and issues have something to do with you.
- Shoulding: Constantly telling yourself you should be doing certain things and criticizing yourself for not doing them.
- Emotional Reasoning: Thinking that if you feel something, it must be true (e.g., "I feel anxious, so I must be in danger." "I feel stupid, so I am stupid.").[11]

Are you susceptible to any of these traps?

Which ones?

Can you give a specific example with an automatic negative thought that was particularly upsetting to you?

Can you see why such traps are often referred to as thinking errors?

I personally tend to fall into the polarizing trap when it comes to my performance. I set very high (too high?) standards for myself and find it difficult to accept anything I perceive as falling short. Being aware of this self-critical tendency does not eliminate it altogether, but it does help me keep it in check to some extent. I also know that this harsh self-critic can lead to unhelpful behaviors.

For example, I am most likely to procrastinate on writing projects (like this book!) because it's rarely good enough for my inner critic. As a wise colleague once told me, "Perfect is the enemy of good." Thinking that what you produce is never quite good enough places you at risk of producing nothing at all. Reminding myself of this truism has helped me get back on track time and time again. In addition to identifying thinking traps, the following strategies can help you challenge and change maladaptive thoughts.

Weigh the Evidence   Subject your automatic thought to the same rigorous process you would use to verify whether something you have heard is true. The court room metaphor [12] can remind you to stick to the facts and weigh all the evidence, as a wise judge would do. When trying a case, the judge and jury listen to both the prosecution and the defense. In this case, a thought that is very upsetting to you is the one on trial. The prosecution brings all the evidence it can muster to support the contention that the thought is entirely true. Then, the defense tries to refute this claim by bringing forth any evidence that this thought or belief is not 100% true. The judge and jury then weigh the evidence and make their judgment.

For the judge to accept this upsetting belief at face value, he or she would have to be convinced that it is entirely true and there is no credible evidence that points to the contrary. If you see that your upsetting thought would not pass this test and be thrown out of court, so to speak, combine the evidence on both sides and come up with a more balanced thought. [13] Try the following exercise.

Write an automatic thought:

_____

_____

What evidence supports the thought?

_____

_____

What evidence does not support the thought?

_____

_____

What is an alternative balanced thought?

_____

_____

A former client of mine at a university counseling center struggled to navigate the social scene in her freshman year. She quickly concluded that she wouldn't be able to make close friends and would end up lonely and isolated. Her evidence was that a girl from her dorm, whom she hoped to be friends with, was aloof when she encountered her in the hallway earlier that morning.

When I asked my client for evidence that does not support her belief, she recounted a pleasant experience working with three other students on an assigned group project. She also told me a guy from her Spanish class suggested they study together for an upcoming test after they commiserated about the heavy workload in the course. We then explored other plausible explanations for the early morning hallway encounter. Could it be that the other student is not a morning person? Or that she slept in and was in a rush to get to class? Examining the evidence led to a more flexible and realistic appraisal of the situation.

Check for Bullying   Years ago, I led a therapy group for women who were struggling with mild to moderate depression. Most of them were highly critical of themselves; their self-talk was replete with putdowns. We did a pair exercise where they were instructed to say to their partner the same critical comments they were saying to themselves. The thought "I will never get this right" had to be phrased as "You will never get this right." "I have no self-control" became "You have no self-control."

Most of the women were highly uncomfortable saying such nasty things to another person. One referred to it as a form of bullying. It was a good reminder that an internal bully should not be tolerated any more than an external one.

Consider your most distressing automatic thought. Would you say this to a friend if she were in a similar situation? Would you say this to your child or someone else you love? What would you say instead? If your thought was said by a bully who is trying to hurt you, what could you say to defend yourself and neutralize the bully?

Consider the Impact   You can evaluate your thought for accuracy, but you can also evaluate it for utility. What are the consequences of thinking this way? Is this thought your friend? Does it help you to think this way, or does it make you feel miserable and keep you stuck?[14] It's also important to consider how your thinking affects your behavior.

You may be avoiding situations that can be stimulating and enjoyable because you worry you won't manage them well. What price are you paying for this avoidance? How can you stand up to your inner bully rather than allow the bully to call the shots and boss you around? At times, automatic thoughts and beliefs can be sticky and resistant to change; however, you don't have to change your thoughts to act in a manner that promotes your health and well-being. In fact, our thoughts can change in a more productive direction as a byproduct of positive experiences.[15]

Modify Your Relationship to Negative Thoughts   Until now our focus has been on challenging and ultimately changing thoughts that fuel distressing emotions and lead to un-helpful behaviors. Since such thoughts are often biased, it stands to reason that altering them can lead to improved moods and more productive actions. But is it really necessary to change your thinking to act more effectively? Do efforts to rid oneself of painful thoughts or replace them with more favorable ones even work? According to a group of approaches known as "third generation" behavior therapy, it is our problematic *relationship* with thoughts, rather than their specific *content*, that creates human suffering.[16]

Our mind cannot help but try to make meaning of events and experiences; this is simply what human minds do. This serves us well when it comes to problem-solving in the external world, where the ability to judge, compare, and predict is indispensable; however, it works less well when applied to the internal life of thoughts and feelings. In fact, attempts to change thoughts and feelings as though they are actual problems encountered in the real world can have the opposite effect of increasing psychological distress.[17] Excessive drinking, illicit drug use, and abuse of prescription medication are often attempts to escape painful thoughts and feelings.

People who habitually procrastinate on important tasks, pass up exciting opportunities, or decline social invitations may be similarly motivated by an urge to avoid negative private experiences. In psychology, this phenomenon is known as experiential avoidance: The urge to avoid internal experiences (thoughts, memories, feelings, sensations) even when doing so is unconstructive in the long run.[18]

When thoughts and feelings are recognized for what they are—mental events that flow through our minds, rather than real entities that have the capacity to harm us—we can accept them rather than struggle to push them away. Your thoughts and emotions, including those that are exceedingly unpleasant, are just thoughts and emotions you are having. If you can accept them as products of your mind rather than literal truths, you can loosen the grip they have on your life.

Instead, you can step back and observe them with curiosity. They are mental events that come and go, and you can let them be, just as they are.[19] Your world is not seen solely through your thoughts if you are aware of yourself as the person doing the thinking. This awareness enables you to look at your thoughts versus through your thoughts.[20]

In a form of counseling known as acceptance commitment therapy (ACT for short)[21], clients learn to **A**ccept their thoughts and feelings, **C**hoose what is important to them, and **T**ake action. Leading the life you want requires taking action that can bring you closer to where you want to go.

At times, the storyteller that is your mind will try to divert you from your path. It will tell you that it's too difficult, that you won't succeed, or that it's best to play it safe. From the perspective of ACT, you don't have to convince yourself that what your mind is telling you is completely false. But neither should you give it the power to control your life and dictate your actions.[22]

The following techniques from the ACT toolbox[23] can help you defuse such thoughts:

1. Bring to mind a negative thought you often have about yourself and that is upsetting to you. Now see what happens if every time you have this thought, you precede it with the following stem: "I am having the thought that . . ." Instead of "I am not smart enough," "I'm having the thought that I'm not smart enough." Instead of "I will feel out of place," "I am having the thought that I will feel out of place." You can add another level to this exercise: "I'm noticing that I'm having the thought that . . ."
2. Bring to mind this or another upsetting and recurring thought. This time, sing it in your head (or out loud if you're alone) to the tune of "Happy Birthday." Alternatively, imagine it coming out of the mouths of some of your favorite cartoon characters.
3. Imagine that the negative chatter in your head is like internet pop-up ads that come out of nowhere and you cannot control. There is no need to click the ads, just let them be.
4. Thank your mind for a thought it continues to pester you with. "Thank you, mind, for telling me that . . ."
5. If your mind is telling you that you can't do something, trick your mind with the following mind game. Say to yourself, "I cannot walk around the room," while at the same time getting up and walking around the room. Warning: Choose something else if you are disabled like me and really can't walk around the room.

The goal of defusing from thoughts is not to change them, make them go away, or believe that they are false. The goal is to make space for them without getting hooked by them. Letting go of the need to change how you think and what you feel can free you up to change what you do. Leading a meaningful and fulfilling life entails taking action that is consistent with your goals and values. Doing so in spite of internal experiences that may suggest otherwise is how new life stories are created.

Write a New Story

We live our lives through stories. Our need to interpret and make meaning of events is simply part of our human DNA. As we link events and experiences across time and make sense of them, we create a story. We have many such stories about our lives. If someone were to ask you about different aspects of your life—your relationships, abilities, passions, struggles, failures, and achievements—you would think about various narratives you have about yourself, stories that were created by linking events together in a particular sequence and giving them meaning. [24] As more and more events are woven together, people develop certain plots and form conclusions about themselves—their capabilities, limitations, and future prospects in various domains of life. They also form conclusions about other people, how they relate to them, and how they compare.

As certain plots and conclusions gain dominance, there is a tendency to select situations that fit them. At the same time, experiences that are unrelated to or inconsistent with these core plots are disregarded. Cognitive behavior therapists refer to such plots as schemas. When certain schemas take hold, they act as filters for incoming information and experiences. Whatever does not fit the schema is either distorted to make it fit or it flies beneath the radar and is altogether ignored. This is why a negative self-schema that one is not competent, worthy, or lovable is so tricky to change; only information that is schema-consistent will be allowed to pass through the filter. [25]

It is important to keep in mind that we do not live in a vacuum. The way we make meaning and the conclusions we come to are influenced by early family life, school and work experiences, and broader social and cultural factors. Your gender, race, sexual orientation, class, and ability status are the contexts within which your stories have developed and are continuing to unfold. This is why the stories we have are not solely our creation; they are shaped by what others have reflected back to us throughout the years and how they have treated us. [26]

A good friend of mine grew up as the daughter of Holocaust survivors. Both her parents have been through the concentration camps and endured the worst imaginable atrocities. They survived and managed to piece their life together and create a family, but their parenting was irreparably damaged by the traumas they had endured.

My friend grew up with little to no affection, along with a daily dose of harsh criticism and putdowns, especially from her mother. The conclusions she formed about herself as a young child continued to impact her as an adult, influencing the decisions she made and the limiting self-stories she at times lived by. Sadly, many children today grow up in families burdened by poverty, violence, and other stressors, which strain their ability to provide a safe and nurturing environment. When such environments are psychologically toxic, children are at risk of developing harmful self-narratives that can limit their present, as well as their future. [27]

While limiting stories can be adopted and reenacted, they can also be edited, reshaped, and reauthored. In narrative therapy, clients learn to let go of damaging narratives and create more empowering and fulfilling ones. They begin to identify exceptions to problems—instances where their actions and interactions did not fit the dominant, deficit oriented-story. [28] In this section, we draw on various approaches and perspectives that demonstrate the ability to reauthor our stories and create new ones that contribute to our well-being.

Isaac's Reauthoring of an Oppressive Childhood Story

Isaac was an eight-year-old boy when his parents were tragically killed in a car accident. He remembers, as if it were yesterday, the moment he learned his mom and dad are never coming back. Along with his older brother and sister, he was staying with family friends while his parents were away on a business trip.

He knew exactly when they were scheduled to return and that something was definitely wrong when they did not. His direct questions about his parents' whereabouts were met with evasive responses by the adults around him. His anxiety grew by the day, until he finally asked to see the local newspaper so that he could check the obituaries. I assume he must have overheard something since asking to read the obituaries is not what you would expect from an eight-year-old child. Needless to say, his request was denied.

Isaac was sitting on the front steps when he saw his 18-year-old cousin Oscar pull into the driveway. Oscar was in the military academy away from home, and in any case, this was not Oscar's house. Another ominous sign. Isaac says that by the time Oscar walked up to him, he knew what he was going to tell him. His parents are dead. Both of them. Isaac and his two siblings would come to live with Oscar's family. Oscar put his hand on Isaac's shoulder and told him he would be okay.

Oscar's mother Chiva, herself a widow, was close to her younger sister Betty, Isaac's mom. She had three teenage children, various health problems, and a modest income. Her elderly mother, who immigrated to Argentina as a young woman but never learned Spanish, lived with her as well. Still, Chiva insisted that she will raise her dead sister's three children, along with her own three. That was the only way to ensure they would not be split apart.

Aunt Chiva passed away many years ago. Isaac wanted me to meet her shortly after the two of us met, and we have some beautiful pictures of her from our wedding more than thirty-five years ago. She did the best she could to provide a safe and nurturing environment for her sister's three orphans. Isaac will be forever grateful for what she did; he dedicated the first book he published to the memory of his parents and aunt.

But at the time, he was a little eight-year-old boy who lost his mom and dad, and whose world was turned upside down overnight. I remember my own fears as a child that something would happen to one of my parents. I can remember having nightmares about that; for Isaac, this nightmare was a reality. In fact, he remembers waking up in the mornings thinking that this was a nightmare, only to realize it was his life.

Not surprisingly, Isaac has very sad childhood memories, despite the loving care he received from his aunt. Importantly, he remembers how burdened he was by the pitying looks he received everywhere he went. He was seen as a *pobrecito*—a poor little soul who everyone felt sorry for. He remembers not wanting to, but being pressured, to go to the home of wealthy distant relatives. The children in the family, whom he did not particularly like, were probably likewise pressured to be nice to the little *pobrecito*.

Isaac was a sad little boy who experienced a horrendous loss; however, his identity as a *pobrecito* emanated from an oppressive story that he was not the author of. This identity weighed him down and exacerbated his grief. In his relationship with his best friend, Beto, Isaac remembers feeling completely free of the burden of this tragic narrative. Beto intuitively knew how to be his friend and show he cared, without the added layer of pity. With Beto, life seemed normal, and Isaac knew he would ultimately be fine, just like Oscar said.

This story is an important part of Isaac's identity. It also speaks to the power stories have in our lives. Isaac knew that the *pobrecito* identity was an oppressive one that he wanted—needed—to distance himself from. And distance himself from it he did. For anyone who knows Isaac as an adult, pity and misfortune are the last things that come to mind. He excelled in soccer and at school, developed close friendships, and emerged as a leader in the youth movement he belonged to. Perhaps, contributing to his community and adding value to the life of others was his way of building a preferred identity and authoring his own story.

Isaac wishes that instead of the *pobrecito* narrative, the adults in his life would have helped him grieve but also highlighted the many strengths he so clearly possessed. It would have helped him know that as difficult and painful as his experience was, it would get better and he would be happy again.

Build on Exceptions and Sparkling Moments

For some people, deficit-oriented and problem-saturated stories become the lens through which they see themselves. Whether these are stories that were started by others or conclusions that they came to themselves, they live by a dominant narrative that privileges events that contribute to the negative plot. Positive examples and sparkling moments that do not fit the negative label are easily missed. Narrative and solution-focused paradigms focus explicitly on exceptions to problem behavior and limiting plots. These exceptions, which are easily overlooked, are the building blocks for more empowering narratives and fulfilling identities. [29]

In my former career as a school psychologist, I attended many school meetings where students that were on my caseload were discussed. Most of these students had various learning and behavioral issues that required a coordinated approach. Unfortunately, such meetings could easily devolve into one example after the next of problem behavior. When the child and the problem are seen as one and the same, the ability to perceive problem-free domains is completely obstructed.

Narrative approaches externalize problems and make the point that the problem is the problem, rather than the person being the problem. It privileges alternative conversations that detail situations when the individual managed to resist the influence of the problem. The more detail that is amassed about healthy exceptions and problem-free domains, the more possible it becomes to create preferred narratives and alternative pathways. [30]

If you are stymied by a problem-saturated narrative that is keeping you stuck, remind yourself that there is more to you than this story and it does not have to define you. This does not mean you are not taking responsibility for your problems. It does mean that you are also able to identify situations where you resisted or limited their impact. Think about one specific situation of standing up to your problem and describe it in detail:

1. When and where did this take place?
2. Who was there?
3. What specifically did you do to resist the problem?
4. What impact did it have on you?
5. Who else benefited from this act of resistance?
6. What enabled you to do this?
7. What does this say about what is important to you and what you stand for?
8. What does it say about who you are as a person?

As someone who lives with a severe physical impairment, asking for help or even accepting it is extremely difficult for me. There are few people that I've allowed to assist me with physical tasks. I wish I could say this has gotten easier throughout the years as I've become more disabled, but to be perfectly honest, it is still a work in progress.

Keep in mind that mainstream society, which exalts independence and denigrates imperfection, has been a historically fertile ground for deficit-oriented and pitying narratives about people with disabilities. The impact of such narratives can be difficult to shake off altogether. Nonetheless, I can identify situations where I've overcome this barrier in the service of important values.

About six years ago, I spearheaded a program for children with disabilities in a boating club in Miami. I would join the kids on excursions in the wheelchair-accessible boat but not go on a sailboat because it required transferring from my wheelchair. My disinclination to let anyone other than Isaac lift me in and out of the boat was stronger than my desire to go on the sailboat. My reluctance was largely due to psychological rather physical discomfort.

Nonetheless, I agreed to do this one day at the urging of an eight-year-old boy who I had grown particularly fond of. Many of the children were there, and I didn't want to perpetuate an oppressive message: that getting help is a sign of weakness or something to be ashamed of. My motivation to demonstrate this enabled me to rise above my own discomfort. Many years before that, on a family trip to the United Kingdom, I had accepted similar help from the driver of a horse-drawn carriage. I could see the eagerness in the eyes of my then-ten-year-old son, as the two of us were strolling the streets of York. Isaac was not with us, and I didn't want to deprive my son of this experience. I'm sure you have your own sparkling moments when you resisted an unhelpful script.

Many people think that to solve a problem or overcome it, it is necessary to explore it in great detail, from multiple perspectives. From a solution-focused viewpoint, the argument is made that this is not always necessary or even helpful. We can learn just as much, or at times even more, by identifying exceptions to problems. It is based on the simple wisdom that one should identify what is already working well and do it more. [31]

Consider what you can learn from your own adaptive responses to difficult situations.

1. When did you behave in unexpected ways to resist the problem or keep it from getting worse?
2. If this was videoed, what would the camera pick up? What would it show you doing?
3. Imagine a scale from 0 to 10, where 0 is the worst the situation has been and 10 is the best the situation has been. What impact did your action have on this scale?

Ultimately, the value of such bright spots and sparkling moments is their ability to inform future courses of action. Thus, it can be helpful to engage in time travel to the future and envision the impact your actions can make.

Imagine that when you go to sleep tonight, a miracle will take place and your problem will go away. Your objective reality will not necessarily change, but it will no longer present a problem for you. Imagine that when you wake up tomorrow morning your problem will be gone, even though you don't know it because you slept through the miracle. [32]

1. What will be different for you in this scenario? How would you know that the problem has gone away?
2. What will you be doing differently? What change in your behavior will be apparent to someone else? What will others do differently?
3. What difference will this make for yourself?
4. What difference will it make for important others?
5. What are some times when a little bit of this miracle is already happening? How can you build on it?

Bolster Resilience

Yesterday afternoon, as I was working on this chapter, I received a WhatsApp call from Isaac's sister Cachi, who lives in Israel. I always enjoy speaking with Cachi, and the two of us are very close. I was particularly moved to speak with her yesterday shortly after I had written about the death of their parents. Cachi, who was twelve years old when her parents died, was a major source of support for her younger brother. Theirs was the only relationship that provided a completely safe space for grieving.

The adults in their lives, in misguided attempts to shield them from pain, placed an implicit yet unmistakable moratorium on grief. They were not taken to their parents' funeral and somehow "knew" that sharing their pain would only make their aunt and grandmother sad. They certainly didn't want to upset the two women who cared for them, so they held on to one another and took their grief underground. Their ability to recover from the tragedy that befell them is a testament to their resilience.

Resilience is defined as healthy adaptation in the face of adversity. When people bounce back and function well in the aftermath of tragedy or other serious challenges, they demonstrate resilience.[33] This speaks to two key factors involved in this process. First, it involves an encounter with a crisis or circumstance that poses a threat to well-being. The death of a loved one, a serious health challenge, the dissolution of a love relationship, or a financial setback are some examples that come to mind. Second, it should be clear that the individual has coped well with this challenging life experience. This doesn't mean we can just walk away unscathed from all forms of tragedy and crisis.

Like Isaac and his family, many people experience emotional upheaval and uncertainty in response to life-changing negative events. The important thing is how they ultimately move beyond it as they continue their life journey.[34]

Some people believe that it is a minority of exceptional people who manage to overcome significant adversity. In fact, we now know it is more accurate to think of resilience as a form of "ordinary magic,"[35] a process most of us are capable of. This is important because everyone can expect to encounter adversity and loss during the course of life.

According to population studies, most people will be exposed to at least one event that is severe enough to meet the criteria for psychological trauma.[36] Whereas such events can pose a threat to well-being, the majority of individuals ultimately recover, adapt, or even grow as a result. How one fares is largely based on an interplay of risk and protective factors within the individual and the environment. A good temperament, psychological flexibility, and strong social skills at the personal level, along with a nurturing and supportive family and a safe community, can play a crucial role in buffering adversity.[37]

Isaac was born into a stable and loving family. Until the accident, when he was eight years old, he lived in a comfortable home with his parents and two siblings. He attended a private Jewish day school and belonged to Hebraica, the Jewish community's country club. There was a lot of anti-Semitism in Argentina at the time, but Isaac was largely sheltered from that as a young child. He was a bright, easygoing, and sociable child with a strong passion for anything soccer.

He loved playing soccer with friends, rooting for "Talleres," his beloved team, and following soccer games on his transistor radio. Isaac was devastated when he lost his parents, and this affected him for years to come. The family savings, needed to support the newly orphaned children, quickly dwindled. He now shared a bedroom with his brother and two male cousins. Finances were tight, and his aunt had to cut corners to support the family of eight: her mother, herself, and the six children.

Isaac's aunt didn't know how to make room for his pain and help him through the grieving process. Nonetheless, she demonstrated her caring in various ways. Money was tight, but there was sufficient food, clean clothes, and an emphasis on education. Isaac remembers doing his homework on the dining room table with his siblings and cousins. He also remembers weekend afternoons with his aunt, the two of them watching old movies on TV, while the older teenagers were out with friends.

Aunt Chiva always had a homemade treat for him to enjoy during the movie. Isaac remembers being sad a lot, but he also knew he was loved. He lived in a safe and structured environment that expected him to succeed. Importantly, the Jewish community enabled him to remain at the school even though the family could no longer afford to pay tuition. He went to school, played soccer, and belonged to a youth movement. There were protective factors within his family and community, in addition to his own skills and assets. The coalescence of these factors contributed to Isaac's excellent adaptation. For children exposed to multiple adversities and insufficient protective buffers, the outcomes are more tenuous.

We know a lot more today about the factors and mechanisms that foster human resilience. In psychology, interest has shifted from profiling a "resilient personality" to developing resilience-bolstering interventions. If anything, it is increasingly clear that the "traits and abilities associated with resilience are part of most people's psychological makeup."[38] There are multiple paths to strengthening resilience, and one size doesn't fit all. People react differently to similar stressful life events and prefer some strategies more than others.[39]

Practicing the well-being skills described in this book can help strengthen your own resilience. We know, for example, that managing strong emotions, acting to solve problems, and reaching out for support are adaptive responses to stressful events. So are keeping things in perspective, questioning negative assumptions, and making room for challenging internal experiences.

The key is to assess the situation you find yourself in and figure out which strategy is most appropriate in this particular circumstance. At times, it's about being attuned to your grief and accepting the pain and heartache that are an inevitable part of our humanity. At other times, it's about seeing the big picture and framing a challenge as a growth-promoting opportunity. Keep in mind that the "doing" is sometimes more important than the "viewing."[40] It's not just about how you frame a situation, but what you do to respond to it. And when you do try something and see that it doesn't work, it's important to be flexible and change course.

The meaning we make of events and the stories we tell about our life will influence our resilience. Whatever doesn't kill us can indeed make us stronger or may even help us thrive. This largely rests on the ability to integrate traumatic events and adverse circumstances into our personal narrative in a health-enhancing manner. In the words of our good friend and eminent psychologist Donald Meichenbaum, "We don't just tell stories, stories tell us."[41] The stories you tell about your life will tell you—to yourself and others. Consider how you can tell affirming narratives of your past that acknowledge mistakes but also honor bright spots. In addition, consider how to turn your values into actions and thus create fulfilling narratives of your present and future.

Act a New Story

"Write a new story" is a metaphor for steering your life in a chosen direction. Whether you choose one direction versus another is based on your values—what you care about and want your life to be about. Ultimately, writing a new story or modifying an existing one requires action. Living according to your values cannot be accomplished by changing how you feel or what you think. It requires acting your way to a new story by aligning daily actions, big and small, with what you want your life to be about.

Values are not the same as goals, although the two are closely related.[42] You may have set a goal to save $500 in the next 30 days to send your child to an art camp. This is a finite goal; you can proudly put it in the "accomplished" bucket if you manage to pull it off. It is likely tied, explicitly or implicitly, to a value you hold about being a good parent. You know it's a value (versus a goal) because it's an ongoing process—something that continues to guide your behavior. You will never claim that you have fully accomplished being a good parent and no longer need to attend to it.

This is particularly relevant in cases where acting in a valued direction entails unpleasant internal experiences that one is motivated to avoid. For example, a parent who is distressed following a recent job loss is highly reluctant to attend his daughter's soccer game. The mere thought of sitting on the bleachers with the other parents and fielding questions about work is anxiety-provoking. Missing the odd game is inconsequential, but you can see why this is a problem if the father's behavior is dictated by the urge to avoid negative thoughts and feelings. If being a good parent is an important value for this father, this may facilitate desired action. He may go to his daughter's soccer game despite his distress because his wish to be there for her trumps the urge to dodge unpleasantness.

Reflecting on your values can help you focus on what you need to do to act on them. This is particularly relevant if you feel stymied by the urge to avoid negative internal experiences. Remember that internal experiences do not need to be managed in the same way as external problems.

It is possible, if not easy, to act in a value-based manner even if doing so involves private experiences you would rather avoid. This is what psychological flexibility is all about.[43] The exercises described earlier for stepping back from such unwanted experiences can facilitate value-driven behavior. In addition, it's worth keeping in mind the added benefits of engaging in a previously avoided behavior. The more you do something, the better you get at it and the greater your sense of mastery and competence. There is pride in resisting your demons and not allowing them to dictate your behavior. Furthermore, acting with purpose makes for a richer, more meaningful life.

THE LAUGHING SIDE

If you want to change a bad habit, you need to pay attention to the thoughts associated with it. Some of the thinking traps are called cognitive errors. Among them, you find "all or none thinking," "minimization," "catastrophizing," and "Fox News." Minimization is pretending that smoking three packs a day is no big deal; that eating donuts for breakfast, lunch, and dinner is better than getting drunk; and that drinking three bottles of rum every night is better than going to the casino, and basically generating a list of more degenerate activities that might make your own degenerate behavior look enlightened.

All or none thinking refers to the proclivity to see the world in black or white with no room for nuance or complexity. This type of thinking, mostly associated with two-year-olds, George W. Bush, and Donald Trump, might lead you to say things like, "You're either with us or against us" or "If I cannot have Hugh Jackman's looks and muscles life is not worth it." I am often tempted to say the latter but am saved from the abyss by my wife the liar, who says I'm beautiful just the way I am.

Thinking leads to narratives, which is a fancy way of saying stories. We all tell stories to ourselves about ourselves. These are often stories of personal defeat. The main thing with thinking is challenging wrong assumptions that are full of cognitive errors. In addition, we need to create new stories about ourselves. For as long as the stories we tell ourselves are full of defeat, dejection, deceit, disillusion, drama, disappointment, and destitution, you pretty quickly run out of D words. On the contrary, if we invent new stories about ourselves, we can make full use of the alphabet: aware, bold, courageous, distinguished, enlightened, friendly, gregarious, humorous, inventive, jovial, kleptomaniac, and so forth.

To make a new story about ourselves, we need to change behaviors and experience positive emotions. What's more, research says the happier you feel the better you become at problem solving, which is not to say that you have to rush to the nearest bar to become more creative. We're talking about natural ways of being happier, for example, reading this book, which is a behavior, something you do. Can you see how it all comes together?

Although there are many ways to synergize behaviors, emotions, and thoughts, research shows conclusively that the best way is to start by buying copies of this book for you and your family, as Christmas and Hanukah presents, as Halloween candy, as Mother's Day and Father's Day gifts, birthday and graduation gifts, bar mitzvah presents, and bris gifts. Just don't read it to the mohel in the middle of the bris.

(Translation: Bris is short for Brit Milah, which is the circumcision of Jewish male newborns that usually takes place on baby's seventh day. Mohel is the person performing the circumcision. This reminds me of so many bris jokes that Ora will never allow me to publish so you will have to come to my next book signing, and I promise to tell you a circumcision joke for every book you buy.)

Catastrophizers and Minimizers Make You Look Normal

Thoughts play tricks on us. On one hand, they may lead us to worry needlessly. We take a pretty mundane concern and turn it into the end of the world. Jewish mothers wrote the book on this. Trust me, I live with one. On the other hand, thoughts may cause us to neglect serious stuff. Overconfident boys wrote the book on this. Believe me, I also have one of those. My wife Ora is a catastrophizer; my son Matan is a minimizer. They make for an interesting life. Best part: They make me look quite normal.

When Matan was young he used to cough. Ora thought it was cystic fibrosis. When the doctor ruled that out, Ora thought it was tuberculosis. When the tests ruled that out, Ora thought it was pertussis. When that was ruled out, Ora moved to another line of worry. Matan is now thirty years old. He recently called us from New York City, where he lives. He reported neck pain. Ora thought it was meningitis.

When Matan was twenty he called Ora from the racquetball court at the university to let her know that a ball had hit him in the eye and he was having trouble seeing. The three of us quickly congregated at home, which is fortunately across the street from the University of Miami. Matan could not only "not see clearly," but also he almost lost his eye. On our way to the hospital, Matan was making jokes that he was going to look like Moshe Dayan, a pretty sexy thing. Ora, meanwhile, was struggling for air. When we arrived at the hospital, the nurses rushed toward Ora, who looked like she was going to faint. Matan, meanwhile, was making jokes.

With parents like us, it is a miracle Matan came out as worry free as he is, which shows he is either someone else's son, genetics is baloney, we did a pretty good job at parenting, or, most likely, he never listened to a word we said. Matan is not only worry free, but also has a marvelous predisposition. He was born happy, optimistic, and with a great sense of humor to boot. Once when he was five years old, we were driving through pastoral Southern Ontario, where we saw lots of cows grazing. He quipped we should rename the country Cownada.

Making lemonade out of lemons is not my strong suit. Ora recently bought tickets for Matan and Elizabeth, his wife, to come to Miami for a few days. After a great visit we drove them back to the airport, only to find out that Ora and I had made a mistake with the tickets and they didn't have a flight to go home that day. Ora and I showed spectacular restraint and fought valiantly the urge to blame one another for the mistake, which we almost did. While we were totally devastated by our incompetence, Matan reconstructed the entire experience as an opportunity to go once more to one of his favorite restaurants in Miami. He radiates positivity, charm, charisma, and warmth, which leads me to think that he probably *is* someone else's kid, which has me really worried now.

Albert Ellis, a famous psychotherapist, used to say that people often engage in *musturbation*: I must do this, I must do that, I must, I must. We *must* ourselves to death. We let our negative thoughts control us and make us miserable. The following is a list of my top musts:

1. I must be loved by everyone.
2. I must leave the house with my clothes on.
3. I must buy life insurance.
4. I must stop worrying.
5. I must stop making lists.
6. I must stop buying brown things.
7. I must get a job with UPS.

Miami, It's Okay; I'm Still Here

Last year rumors spread about Beckham leaving Miami and going to Broward County to find a location for his soccer stadium. Soon after that, LeBron James announced he was going back to the Cleveland Cavaliers. I know you're all thinking that I'm next, that Miami does not measure up to the likes of Beckham, James, and Prilleltensky, the great three; but I want to reassure you that I have rejected offers to return to Argentina to head a paramilitary group to hunt down international creditors.

This is an opportunity for Miami to turn inward, to resist the limelight, to become a more down-to-earth place—a place of contemplation and introspection. It's time to look at our inner beauty. In short, it's time to write a new story about Miami. I know that deep down, beneath several inches of silicon, augmented breasts and Brazilian butt lifts, we all want to lead a simple life, devoid of capricious celebrities without loyalty.

But it's no time to be judgmental Miami. It's time to be compassionate. After all, most of us came here from somewhere else. Many of us have experienced separations before, from a nasty divorce, bankruptcy, communism, death squads, or tax collectors up north. Of all people, Miamians should understand LeBron wanting to go home. After all, we have here hundreds of thousands of people who want to return to their home. It's no time to be angry Miami; it's time to celebrate what we do have:

1. We still have the most drivers with a disability placard who get out of their cars miraculously cured, with no apparent sign of physical impairment. All you have to do in Miami to overcome a physical disability is get one of those placards from your uncle's deceased neighbor in Little Havana. As soon as you put it in your car, you're cured. Try it. I have seen thousands of people in Miami park their cars in handicapped-reserved spots and sprint out of the car like they've never had a disability in their lives.
2. We're still the most bureaucracy-free health care delivery system in the nation, otherwise known as America's Medicare fraud capital.

3. We're still the only major city in the United States without a prefrontal cortex. People here are devoid of inhibitions and accompanying neuroses. We're the least repressed city in the world, saving us millions of dollars in costly psychiatric and psychological treatments. Only here do people continue to build near the shoreline as if climate change happens just in English-speaking parts of the country. Only a cortex-free city does that.

4. We still have the most creative drivers in United States, who stop their cars in the middle of the road for no apparent reason other than to contemplate the beautiful surroundings or text their *abuelita*. To optimize brain flexibility, drivers here never signal, keeping you guessing and forcing you to perform maneuvers you only see in commercials displaying the disclaimer "professional driver featured."

5. We still have the most inflated real estate market in the universe, where the only people able to afford a condo live 7,500 miles away and pay with cash obtained in dubious circumstances.

6. We're still the only major city where people are allowed to text and drive. Here you don't have to pay attention to traffic rules. Here you're free of government intervention into your personal affairs. Only here you can decide when you want to seal a deal via text. Try texting and driving in other major cities in the United States and the police will get between you and your hard-fought liberties.

7. We're still the only city where taxpayers subsidize millionaire sports club owners. Beckham will return once the mayor and city commissioners return to their senses (which he did in the summer of 2015; I knew it!).

8. We're still the only city in the world where 93% of the population says *pero* instead of "but," enriching the cultural experience of visitors and residents alike.

9. We're still the city with the most implanted silicon per anatomical square inch in the world. Try that, Cleveland!

Keep your head up Miami. We have nothing to fear. I'm still here.

Notes

PREFACE

1. Cann, A., & Kuiper, N. A. (2014). Research on the role of humor in well-being and health. *Europe's Journal of Psychology, 10,* 412–28. DOI:10.5964/ejop.v10i3.818; Cann, A., & Collette, C. (2014). Sense of humor, stable affect, and psychological well-being. *Europe's Journal of Psychology, 10,* 464–79. DOI:10.5964/ejop.v10i3.746; Crawford, S. A., & Caltabiano, N. J. (2011). Promoting emotional well-being through the use of humor. *Journal of Positive Psychology, 6,* 237–52. DOI:10.1080/17439760.2011.577087; Maiolino, N. B., & Kuiper, N.A. (2016). Examining the impact of a brief humor exercise on psychological well-being. *Translational Issues in Psychological Science, 2*(1), 4–13. DOI:10.1037/tps0000065.
2. Prilleltensky, I. (2016). *The laughing guide to well-being: Using humor and science to become happier and healthier.* Lanham, MD: Rowman & Littlefield.

1. DRIVERS OF CHANGE

1. Duhigg, C. (2014). *The power of habit.* New York: Random House.
2. Fredrickson, B. A. (2009). *Positivity.* New York: Three Rivers; Fredrickson, B. A., & Kurtz, L. (2011). Cultivating positive emotions to enhance human flourishing. In S. I. Donaldson, M. Csikszentmihalyi, & J. Nakamura (eds.), *Applied positive psychology: Improving everyday life, health, schools, work, and society* (pp. 35–47). New York: Routledge.
3. Dweck, C. S. (2006). *Mindset: The new psychology of success.* New York: Random House.

2. BEHAVIORS

1. Norcross, J. C. (2012). *Changeology: Five steps to realizing your goals and resolutions.* New York: Simon & Schuster; Watson, D. L., & Tharp, R. G. (2014). *Self-directed behavior: Self-modification for personal adjustment* (10th ed.). Belmont, CA: Cengage Learning.
2. Dolan, P. (2014). *Happiness by design: Change what you do, not how you feel.* New York: Penguin.
3. Sheldon, K. M. (2014). Becoming oneself: The central role of self-concordant goal selection. *Personality and Social Psychology Review, 18*(4), 349–65; Sheldon, K. M, & Elliot, A. J. (1999). Goal striving, need-satisfaction, and longitudinal well-being: The self-concordance model. *Journal of Personality and Social Psychology, 76,* 482–97.
4. Adriaanse, M. A., Gollwitzer, P. M., De Ridder, D. T. D., De Wit, J. B. F., & Kroese, F. M. (2011). Breaking habits with implementation intentions: A test of underlying processes. *Personality and Social Psychology Bulletin, 37,* 502–513. DOI:10.1177/0146167211399102.
5. Koestner, R., Lekes, N., Powers, T. A., & Chicoine, E. (2002). Attaining personal goals: Self-concordance plus implementation intentions equals success. *Journal of Personality and Social Psychology, 83*(1), 231–44. DOI:10.1037//0022-3514.83.1.2315; Sheldon, Becoming oneself.

6. Watson & Tharp, *Self-directed behavior.*

7. Norcross, *Changeology.*

8. Norcross, *Changeology*; Watson & Tharp, *Self-directed behavior.*

9. Conzemius, A., O'Neill, J., & Commodore, C. (2005). *The power of SMART goals.* Bloomington, IN: Solution Tree.

10. Koestner, Lekes, Powers, & Chicoine, Attaining personal goals.

11. Achtziger, A., Gollwitzer, P. M., & Sheeran, P. (2008). Implementation intentions and shielding goal striving from unwanted thoughts and feelings. *Personality and Social Psychology Bulletin, 34*(3), 381–93. DOI:10.1177/0146167207311201.

12. Adriaanse, Gollwitzer, De Ridder, De Wit, & Kroese, Breaking habits with implementation intentions; Gollwitzer, P. M. (1999). Implementation intentions: Strong effects of simple plans. *American Psychologist, 54*(7), 493–503. DOI:10.1037/0003-066X.54.7.493; Koestner, Lekes, Powers, & Chicoine, Attaining personal goals.

13. Gollwitzer, P. M. (2014). Weakness of the will: Is a quick fix possible? *Motivation and Emotion, 38*(3), 305–22. DOI:10.1007/s11031-014-9416-3; Gollwitzer, Implementation intentions.

14. Adriaanse, Gollwitzer, De Ridder, De Wit, & Kroese, Breaking habits with implementation intentions; Friedman, S., & Ronen, S. (2015). The effect of implementation intentions on transfer of training. *European Journal of Social Psychology, 45*(4), 409–16. DOI:10.1002/ejsp.2114.

15. Oettingen, G. (2014*). Rethinking positive thinking: Inside the new science of motivation.* New York: Current.

16. Greiner, K. A., Daley, C. M., Epp, A., James, A., Yeh, H., Geana, M., & Ellerbeck, E. F. (2014). Implementation intentions and colorectal screening. *American Journal of Preventive Medicine, 47*(6), 703–14. DOI:10.1016/j.amepre.2014.08.005.

17. Gollwitzer, P. M., & Sheeran, P. (2006). Implementation intentions and goal achievement: A meta-analysis of effects and processes. *Advances in Experimental Social Psychology, 38*, 69–119.

18. Gollwitzer, Implementation intentions.

19. McGonigal, K. (2012). *The willpower instinct: Why self-control works, why it matters, and how you can get more of it.* New York: Penguin.

20. Oettingen, *Rethinking positive thinking.*

21. Mischel, W., Shoda, Y., & Rodriguez, M. (1989). Delay of gratification in children. *Science*, 244 , 933–38. DOI:10.1126/science.2658056.

22. McGonigal, *The willpower instinct.*

23. Watson & Tharp, *Self-directed behavior.*

24. Norcross, *Changeology*; Watson & Tharp, *Self-directed behavior.*

25. Norcross, *Changeology*; Watson & Tharp, *Self-directed behavior.*

26. McGonigal, *The willpower instinct.*

27. Bandura, A. (1997). *Self-efficacy: The exercise of control.* New York: Freeman.

28. Watson & Tharp, *Self-directed behavior.*

29. Norcross, *Changeology.*

30. Watson & Tharp, *Self-directed behavior.*

31. Norcross, *Changeology.*

32. Arieli, D. (2009). *Predictably irrational: The hidden forces that shape our decisions.* New York: HarperCollins.

33. Watson & Tharp, *Self-directed behavior.*

34. Norcross, *Changeology*; Watson & Tharp, *Self-directed behavior.*

35. Koestner, Lekes, Powers, & Chicoine, Attaining personal goals.

36. Wansink, B. (2014). *Slim by design: Mindless eating solutions.* New York: HarperCollins.

37. Norcross, *Changeology.*

38. Rath, T., & Harter, J. (2010). *Well-Being: The five essential elements.* New York: Gallup Press.

39. Norcross, *Changeology.*

40. McGonigal, *The willpower instinct.*

41. Arieli, *Predictably irrational.*

42. Norcross, *Changeology.*

43. McGonigal, *The willpower instinct.*

3. EMOTIONS

1. Lyubomirsky, S., Sheldon, K., & Schkade, D. (2005). Pursuing happiness: The architecture of sustainable change. *Review of General Psychology, 9*(2), 111–31.

2. Diener, E., & Biswas-Diener, R. (2008). *Happiness: Unlocking the mysteries of psychological wealth.* Malden, MA: Blackwell; Fredrickson, B. (2004). The broaden-and-build theory of positive emotions. *Philosophical Transactions of the Royal Society B: Biological Sciences, 359*(1449), 1,367–77; Gloria, C., & Steinhardt, M. (2016). Relationships among positive emotions, coping, resilience, and mental health. *Stress and Health, 32*(2), 145–56.

3. Danner, D. D., Snowdon, D. A., & Friesen, W. V. (2001). Positive emotions in early life and longevity: Findings from the nun study. *Journal of Personality and Social Psychology, 80*(5), 804–13.

4. Danner, Snowdon, & Friesen, Positive emotions in early life and longevity; Diener & Biswas-Diener, *Happiness*.

5. Cohen, S., Tyrrell, D., & Smith, A. (1991). Psychological stress and susceptibility to the common cold. *New England Journal of Medicine, 325*(9), 606–12.

6. Boehm, J., & Kubzansky, L. (2012). The heart's content: The association between positive psychological well-being and cardiovascular health. *Psychological Bulletin, 138*(4), 655–91.

7. Fredrickson, The broaden-and-build theory of positive emotions; Gloria & Steinhardt, Relationships among positive emotions, coping, resilience, and mental health.

8. Bandura, A. (1997). *Self-efficacy: The exercise of control.* New York: Freeman.

9. Catalino, L., & Fredrickson, B. (2011). A Tuesday in the life of a flourisher: The role of positive emotional reactivity in optimal mental health. *Emotion, 11*(4), 938–50; Fredrickson, B. A. (2009). *Positivity.* New York: Three Rivers.

10. Diener & Biswas-Diener, *Happiness*.

11. Baumgardner, R., & Crothers, M. (2009). *Positive psychology.* Upper Saddle River, NJ: Prentice Hall; Day, J. M. (2017). Religion and human development in adulthood: Well-being, prosocial behavior, and religious and spiritual development. *Behavioral Development Bulletin, 22*(2), 298–313. DOI:10.1037/bdb0000031.

12. Seligman, M. (2011). *Flourish: A visionary new understanding of happiness and well-being.* New York: Free Press.

13. Dolan, P. (2014). *Happiness by design: Change what you do, not how you think.* New York: Penguin; Fredrickson, B. A., & Kurtz, L. (2011). Cultivating positive emotions to enhance human flourishing. In S. I. Donaldson, M. Csikszentmihalyi, & J. Nakamura (eds.), *Applied positive psychology: Improving everyday life, health, schools, work, and society* (pp. 35–47). New York: Routledge.

14. Baumgardner & Crothers, *Positive psychology*.

15. Diener, E. (2015). Why people are in a generally good mood. *Personality and Social Psychology Review, 19*(3), 235–56.

16. Fredrickson, B. (2013). Updated thinking on positivity ratios. *American Psychologist, 68*(9), 814–22.

17. Biswas-Diener, R. (2010). *Practicing positive psychology coaching.* Hoboken, NJ: John Wiley & Sons.

18. Seligman, M., Steen, T., Park, N., & Peterson, C. (2005). Positive psychology progress: Empirical validation of interventions. *American Psychologist, 60*(5), 410–21.

19. Arakawa, D., & Greenburg, M. (2007). Optimistic managers and their influence on productivity and employee engagement in a technology organization: Implications for coaching psychologists. *International Coaching Psychology Review, 2*, 78–89.

20. Biswas-Diener, *Practicing positive psychology coaching*.

21. Lomas, T., Froh, J. J., Emmons, R. A., & Mishra, A. (2014). Gratitude interventions: A review and future agenda. In A. Parks & Stephen M. Schueller (eds.), *Handbook of positive psychological interventions* (pp. 3–19). Maiden, MA: Wiley-Blackwell.

22. Emmons, R. A., & McCullough, M. E. (2003). Counting blessings versus burdens: An experimental investigation of gratitude and subjective well-being in daily life. *Journal of Personality and Social Psychology, 84*(2), 377–89. DOI:10.1037/0022- 3514.84.2.377.

23. Seligman, Steen, Park, & Peterson, Positive psychology progress.

24. Lyubomirsky, S. (2011). Hedonic adaptation to positive and negative experiences. In S. Folkman (ed.), *Oxford handbook of stress, health, and coping* (pp. 200–24). New York: Oxford University Press.

25. Bryant, F., & Veroff, J. (2006). *Savoring: A new model of positive experience.* Mahwah, NJ: Earlbaum.

26. Lyubomirsky, S. (2007). *The how of happiness: The new approach to getting the life you want.* New York: Penguin; Sheldon, K., & Lyubomirsky, S. (2012). The challenge of staying happier. *Personality and Social Psychology Bulletin, 38*(5), 670–80.

27. Lyubomirsky, Hedonic adaptation to positive and negative experiences.

28. Smith, J. L., Harrison, P. R., Kurtz, J. L., & Bryant, F. B. (2014). Nurturing the capacity to savor: Interventions to enhance the enjoyment of positive experiences. In A. C. Parks & S. M. Schueller (eds.), *The Wiley-Blackwell handbook of positive psychological interventions* (pp. 42–65). Hoboken, NJ: Wiley-Blackwell.

29. Slotter, E., & Ward, D. (2015). Finding the silver lining. *Journal of Social and Personal Relationships, 32*(6), 737–56.

30. Roepke, A., & Nezu, A. M. (2015). Psychosocial interventions and posttraumatic growth: A meta-analysis. *Journal of Consulting and Clinical Psychology, 83*(1), 129–42.

31. Bower, J., Moskowitz, J., & Epel, E. (2009). Is benefit finding good for your health? *Current Directions in Psychological Science, 18*(6), 337–41.

32. Brackett, M. A., Rivers, S. E., & Salovey, P. (2011). Emotional intelligence: Implications for personal, social, academic, and workplace success. *Social and Personality Psychology Compass, 5*, 88–103; Brackett, M. A., Mayer, J. D., & Warner, R. M. (2004). Emotional intelligence and its relation to everyday behavior. *Personality and Individual Differences, 36*, 1,387–1,402.

33. Kashdan, T., Barrett, L., & McKnight, P. (2015). Unpacking emotion differentiation. *Current Directions in Psychological Science, 24*(1), 10–16; Werner, K., & Gross, J. J. (2010). Emotion regulation and psychopathology: A

conceptual framework. In A. M. Kring & D. M. Sloan (eds.), *Emotion regulation and psychopathology: A transdiagnostic approach to etiology and treatment* (pp. 13–37). New York: Guilford.

34. Nolen-Hoeksema, S., Wisco, B., & Lyubomirsky, S. (2008). Rethinking rumination. *Perspectives on Psychological Science, 3*(5), 400–424; Zawadzki, M. (2015). Rumination is independently associated with poor psychological health: Comparing emotion regulation strategies. *Psychology & Health,* 1–36.

35. Garland, E. L., Fredrickson, B., Kring, A. M., Johnson, D. P., Meyer, P. S., & Penn, D. L. (2010). Upward spirals of positive emotions counter downward spirals of negativity: Insights from the broaden-and-build theory and affective neuroscience on the treatment of emotion dysfunctions and deficits in psychopathology. *Clinical Psychology Review, 30*(7), 849–64; Lyubomirsky, *The how of happiness.*

36. Gross, J. (ed.). (2014). *Handbook of emotion regulation* (2nd. ed.). New York, NY: Guilford.

37. Watson, D. L., & Tharp, R. G. (2014). *Self-directed behavior: Self-modification for personal adjustment* (10th ed.). Belmont, CA: Cengage Learning.

38. Germer, C., & Neff, K. (2013). Self-compassion in clinical practice. *Journal of Clinical Psychology, 69*(8), 856–67; Neff, K. D., Rude, S. S., & Kirkpatrick, K. L. (2007). An examination of self-compassion in relation to positive psychological functioning and personality traits. *Journal of Research and Personality, 41,* 908–16.

39. Germer & Neff, Self-compassion in clinical practice; Neff, Rude, & Kirkpatrick, An examination of self-compassion in relation to positive psychological functioning and personality traits.

40. Harris, R. (2009). *ACT made simple: An easy-to-read primer on acceptance and commitment therapy.* Oakland, CA: New Harbinger Publications.

41. Biglan, A., Hayes, S., & Pistorello, C. (2008). Acceptance and commitment: Implications for prevention science. *Prevention Science, 9*(3), 139–52; Biglan, A. (2015). *The nurture effect: How the science of human behavior can improve our lives and our world* . Oakland, CA: New Harbinger Publications.

42. Bushman, B. J. (2002). Does venting anger feed or extinguish the flame? Catharsis, rumination, distraction, anger, and aggressive responding. *Personality and Social Psychology Bulletin, 28,* 724–31.

43. Heppner, P., Witty, T., & Dixon, W. (2004). Problem-solving appraisal and human adjustment: A review of twenty years of research using the problem-solving inventory. *Counseling Psychologist, 32*(3), 344–428; Weiten, W., Dunn, D., & Yost Hammer, E. (2012). *Psychology applied to modern life: Adjustment in the 21st century* (10th ed.). Belmont, CA: Wadsworth/Cengage Learning.

44. Bonanno, G., & Burton, C. (2013). Regulatory flexibility. *Perspectives on Psychological Science, 8*(6), 591–612.

45. Weiten, Dunn, & Yost Hammer, *Psychology applied to modern life.*

46. Ryff, C. (2014). Psychological well-being revisited: Advances in the science and practice of eudaimonia. *Psychotherapy and Psychosomatics, 83*(1), 10–28.

4. THOUGHTS

1. Dobson, D., & Dobson, K. S. (2009). *Evidence-based practice of cognitive-behavioral therapy.* New York: Guilford.

2. Hayes, S. C., Strosahl, K. D., & Wilson, K. G. (2012). *Acceptance and commitment therapy* (2nd ed.). New York: Guilford.

3. Beck, A., & Haigh, E. (2014). Advances in cognitive theory and therapy: The generic cognitive model. *Annual Review of Clinical Psychology, 10,* 1–24.

4. Beck, J. S. (2011). *Cognitive behavior therapy: Basics and beyond* (2nd ed.). New York: Guilford.

5. Hays, P. (2014). *Creating well-being: Four steps to a happier, healthier life.* Washington, DC: American Psychological Association.

6. Dobson & Dobson, *Evidence-based practice of cognitive-behavioral therapy*; Greenberger, D., & Padesky, C. (1995). *Mind over mood: Changing how you feel by changing the way you think.* New York: Guilford.

7. Belloch, A., Morillo, C., Lucero, M., Cabedo, E., & Carrió, C. (2004). Intrusive thoughts in nonclinical subjects: The role of frequency and unpleasantness on appraisal ratings and control strategies. *Clinical Psychology & Psychotherapy, 11,* 100–110.

8. O'Donohue, W., & Fisher, J. (2012). *Cognitive behavior therapy: Core principles for practice.* Hoboken, NJ: John Wiley & Sons; Larsson, A., Hooper, N., Osborne, L., Bennett, P., & McHugh, L. (2016). Using brief cognitive restructuring and cognitive defusion techniques to cope with negative thoughts. *Behavior Modification, 40*(3), 452–82.

9. Leahy, R. L., & Rego, S. A. (2012) Cognitive restructuring. In W. O'Donohue & J. E. Fisher (eds.), *Cognitive behavior therapy: Core principles for practice* (pp. 133–58). Hoboken, NJ: John Wiley & Sons.

10. Beck, *Cognitive behavior therapy.*

11. Burns, D. (1999). *Ten days to self-esteem.* New York: Quill; DeRubeis, R. J., Webb, C. A., Tang, T. Z., & Beck, A. T. (2010). Cognitive therapy. In K. S. Dobson (ed.), *Handbook of cognitive-behavioral therapies* (3rd ed.). (pp. 277–316). New York: Guilford; Greenberger & Padesky, *Mind over mood.*

12. Leahy & Rego, Cognitive restructuring.

13. O'Donohue, W., & Fisher, J. E. (eds.). (2012). *Cognitive behavior therapy: Core principles for practice.* Hoboken, NJ: John Wiley & Sons.

14. Leahy & Rego, Cognitive restructuring.

15. Beck, *Cognitive behavior therapy.*

16. Hayes, S. C., Luoma, J. B., Bond, F. W., Masuda, A., & Lillis, J. (2006). Acceptance and commitment therapy: Model, processes, and outcomes. *Behaviour Research and Therapy, 44*(1), 1–25.

17. Biglan, A., Hayes, S., & Pistorello, C. (2008). Acceptance and commitment: Implications for Prevention Science. *Prevention Science, 9*(3), 139–52.

18. Hayes, Strosahl, & Wilson, *Acceptance and commitment therapy*; Hayes, S., & Smith, S. (2005). *Get out of your mind and into your life: The new acceptance and commitment therapy.* Oakland, CA: New Harbinger Publications.

19. Harris, R. (2009). *ACT made simple: An easy-to-read primer on acceptance and commitment therapy.* Oakland, CA: New Harbinger Publications.

20. Hayes & Smith, *Get out of your mind and into your life.*

21. Harris, R. (2011). *The confidence gap: A guide to overcoming fear and self-doubt.* Boulder, CO: Trumpeter Books.

22. Harris, *ACT made simple.*

23. Hayes, Strosahl, & Wilson, *Acceptance and commitment therapy*; Larsson, Hooper, Osborne, Bennett, & McHugh, Using brief cognitive restructuring and cognitive defusion techniques to cope with negative thoughts.

24. Morgan, A. (2000). *What is narrative therapy?* Adelaide, South Australia: Dulwich Center Publications.

25. Beck, *Cognitive behavior therapy.*

26. Combs, G., & Freedman, J. (2012). Narrative, post-structuralism, and social justice: Current practices in narrative therapy. *Counseling Psychologist, 40*, 1,033–60; Morgan, *What is narrative therapy?*

27. Biglan, A. (2015). *The nurture effect: How the science of human behavior can improve our lives and our world.* Oakland, CA: New Horizons; Putnam, R. D. (2015). *Our kids: The American dream in crisis.* New York: Simon & Schuster.

28. Pals, J. L. (2006). Narrative identity processing of difficult life experiences: Pathways of personality development and positive self-transformation in adulthood. *Journal of Personality, 74*, 1,079–110; White, M., & Epston, D. (1990). *Narrative means to therapeutic ends* (1st ed.). New York: W. W. Norton.

29. McLean, K. C., Pasupathi, M., & Pals, J. L. (2007). Selves creating stories creating selves: A process of self-development. *Personality and Social Psychology Review, 11*, 262–78. DOI:10.1177/1088868307301034; Morgan, *What is narrative therapy?*

30. Morgan, *What is narrative therapy?*; White & Epston, *Narrative means to therapeutic ends.*

31. Bannink, F. P. (2014). Positive CBT: From reducing distress to building success. *Journal of Contemporary Psychotherapy, 44*(1), 1–8; Bannink, F. P., & Jackson, P. Z. (2011). Positive psychology and solution focus: Looking at similarities and differences. *InterAction, 3* (1), 8–20.

32. Bannink, F. P. (2012). *Practicing positive CBT: From reducing distress to building success.* Hoboken, NJ: John Wiley & Sons.

33. Meichenbaum, D. (2012). *A roadmap to resilience.* Clearwater, FL: Institute Press.

34. Baumgardner, R., & Crothers, M. (2009). *Positive psychology.* Upper Saddle River, NJ: Prentice Hall.

35. Masten, A. (2001). Ordinary magic: Resilient processes and development. *American Psychologist, 56*, 227–38.

36. Bonanno, G., Westphal, M., & Mancini, A. (2011.). Resilience to loss and potential trauma. *Annual Review of Clinical Psychology, 7*, 511–35; Substance Abuse and Mental Health Services Administration. (2012). *Behavioral health, United States, 2012.* Retrieved from http://www.samhsa.gov/data/sites/default/files/2012-BHUS.pdf

37. Masten, Ordinary magic.

38. Baumgardner & Crothers, *Positive psychology.*

39. The road to resilience, *American Psychological Association*, http://www.apa.org/helpcenter/road-resilience/aspx.

40. O'Hanlon, B. (2000). *Do one thing different.* New York: HarperCollins.

41. Meichenbaum, *A roadmap to resilience*, 138.

42. Harris, *ACT made simple*; Harris, *The confidence gap.*

43. Biglan, Hayes, & Pistorello, Acceptance and commitment.

Index

acceptance commitment therapy (ACT), 64
adversity: resilience and, 69–70; silver linings and, 42–43
"aha moments", 58
Alcoholics Anonymous, 52
all or none thinking, 71
alternatives: diet options, 21, 25; exploring, 21
ambivalence, 9–10
anger, 4, 60
anticipation, 41–42
anxiety, 49, 58, 60
Argentina and soccer, 54–55
Arieli, Dan, 19
attainable goals. *See* SMART goals
attitudes. *See* thoughts
Australia story, 3
avoidance, 64, 71

Beck, Aaron, 58
behaviors: about, 1, 2; controlling despite emotions, 49; costs and benefits of changing, 10; as driver of change, 28; habits and, 15–16; laughing side, 25–29; as learned skills, 7; neurosis controlled with, 4; positive habits, 14–15; reinforcing, 16–17, 19–20; rewarding yourself for, 16; triggers, 16, 17. *See also* goals; obstacles to behavior change
beliefs. *See* thoughts
broaden-and-build theory, 32
broad perspective, 32–33
bullying behavior, 63

catastrophizers, 72
Catholic nuns study, 32, 33
challenges and silver linings, 42–43
change: "cold turkey", 18, 25; costs and benefits of, 10; drivers of, 1–2; in goals, 27; health improvements and, 25; pros and cons, 26–27. *See*

also alternatives; behaviors; emotions; GREASE strategies; thoughts
chess, passion for, 41
childhood grief, 66–67, 69–70
cognitive errors, 71
"cold turkey" change, 18, 25
community, sense of, 33
compliments, 20
computer charger story, 59–61
connections in relationships, 33
coping strategies, 43–45
court room metaphor, 62–63

delayed gratification, 14–15
depression, 34–35
disability stories, 41, 67–68
dopamine, 16

eating habits: diet options, 21, 25; as habit, 28–29; mindlessness in, 20; prebeaning, 20, 27; self-compassion and, 48
Ellis, Albert, 58, 73
emotions: about, 1, 2; assessing, 49; happiness continuum, 31; laughing side, 52–55; male emotional brain in garage, 4–5; pleasure and purpose, 33–34; understanding, 45–47. *See also* negative emotions; positive emotions
Epictetus, 57
eudaimonic positive emotions, 54
evidence of thoughts, 62–63
exceptions, 67–68
exercises: anticipating future events, 41–42; choosing good goals, 7–9; coping strategies, 44–45, 49–51; costs and benefits of changing behaviors, 10; finding pleasure and purpose, 33–34; gratitude journal, 39; interactions of behaviors, emotions and thoughts, 46–47; overcoming barriers, 13–14; problem-saturated

self-control: education and, 23–25; issues causing failure, 24; marshmallow experiment, 14–15
self-deprecation, 27
self-rewards, 18–20
serenity prayer, 52
Shakespeare, William, 57
silver linings, 42–43
SMART goals, 11, 27–28
social circle support, 21–23
specific goals. *See* SMART goals
spirituality, 33
stories: acting a new story, 70–71; childhood grief, 66–67, 69–70; cognitive errors and, 71; influenced by early life, 65; Miami stories, 73–74; narratives, 71–72; narrative therapy, 65; resilience bolstered by, 69–70; schemas as, 65
studying habits, 20–21
suffering, acknowledgement of, 48
"third generation" behavior therapy, 63

thoughts: about, 1, 2; actions and emotions affected by, 57, 60; challenging negative emotions, 61–64; computer charger story, 59–61; defusing with ACT toolbox, 64; evaluating utility of, 63; faulty appraisals, 58–59; laughing side, 71–74; negativity, 59–61; tracking, 60, 60–61. *See also* fight or flight response; stories
time-bound goals. *See* SMART goals
toolbox for ACT, 64
toolbox metaphor, 45
twelve-step programs, 52

values, 71

weaknesses, 35
what the hell effect, 24
willpower, 25, 28
The Willpower Instinct (McGonigal), 24

About the Authors

Dr. Isaac Prilleltensky is former dean of the School of Education and Human Development at the University of Miami, where he currently serves as vice provost for institutional culture. He also holds the Erwin and Barbara Mautner Chair in Community Well-Being, and is professor of educational and psychological studies. He has published eight books and more than 130 scholarly papers, book chapters, and book reviews. He is the recipient of the Distinguished Contribution to Theory and Research Award, and the John Kalafat Applied Community Psychology Award, both from the Division of Community Psychology of the American Psychological Association (APA). He is also the recipient of the Lifetime Achievement Award of the Prevention Section of the Division of Counseling Psychology of APA. In 2015, he received an award from the National Newspaper Association for his humor writing. Isaac was born in Argentina and has lived and worked in Israel, Canada, Australia, and the United States. He lives in Miami with his amazing wife, Dr. Ora Prilleltensky. Their son Matan lives in New York City. Isaac can be reach at isaac@miami.edu.

Ora Prilleltensky obtained her doctorate in Counseling Psychology from OISE at the University of Toronto. She is former director of the major in human and social development at the University of Miami and has taught various graduate and undergraduate courses. Prior to moving to Miami, Ora taught at Vanderbilt's Peabody College. She has also worked in a variety of clinical settings, including a child guidance clinic, a university counseling center, and a rehabilitation hospital. Ora has muscular dystrophy and uses a power wheelchair. Her research interests include disability studies and the promotion of well-being. She is author of *Motherhood and Disability: Children and Choices* and coauthor of *Promoting Well-Being: Linking Personal, Organizational, and Community Change*. Ora is on the board of Research and Reform for Children in Court. She has also served on Miami-Dade County's Commission on Disability Issues. She can be reached at ora@miami.edu.